Ballad of BAPU

Santosh Bakaya

Vitasta

Let Knowledge Spread

Published by
Renu Kaul Verma
Vitasta Publishing Pvt Ltd
2/15, Ansari Road, Daryaganj
New Delhi - 110 002
info@vitastapublishing.com

ISBN 978-93-82711-57-5

First Edition 2015
Third Reprint 2020
MRP: ₹ 495

Typeset by Vits Press
Printed by Thomson Press (India) Ltd.

Contents

My Life is my Message

For my Mother

You suddenly left us on that cold morning of 9 January 2015. But no, you did not go. Your resilience and never-say-die spirit still prods us on.

'As a mother, my heart beats in five different places, in my five children', you used to say. Yes, it still beats on with the same never-say-die spirit in each one of us. No, you have not gone.

That effulgent ember that still lights up the dark nights, that irrepressible laughter that still scintillates, that wit which still sparkles and that incredible humour which still tickles, is it not yours? No, you are not gone.

And I am not in denial.

'When is the book launch?' you asked me in that last phone call.

You were keen on this book, so this book is for you, Mummy.

With all my love.

Gandhi leading the Dandi march

Acknowledgements

To my dearest friend, Joyce Yarrow, a big thank you and a bigger hug for her constant nudges, her insightful comments and her wonderful friendship.

And for sharing this roller-coaster ride with me, a huge thank you from the bottom of my heart to my husband, Lalit, and my daughter Iha, who have all along endured my tantrums and also discreetly steered clear of me when I have been in one of my so-called creative phases.

Thank you, Renu Kaul Verma, my publisher, and my editor, Papri Sri Raman, for your faith in me.

A special and heartfelt thanks to my dear friends, Ampat Koshy and Abhijit Basu, for magnanimously lending those last -minute touches which enriched both me and the manuscript.

All photographs of the times, Mahatma Gandhi's and other leaders' pictures have been accessed from the internet and acknowledged to Creative Commons resources shared for educational purposes. The photographs are more than sixty years old and their clarity cannot be controlled.

Mahatma Gandhi's father Karamchand Gandhi

Mahatma Gandhi's mother Putlibai

Foreword

As a poet and an American professor of peace building, I am honored and happy to write this foreword for Santosh Bakaya's poetic biography of the greatest peace builder the world has ever known: Gandhi. How fitting that this biography is written as poems.

Gandhi has inspired so many generations around the world and continues to do so with his 'mere words', or profoundly relevant phrases like 'we need to be the change we wish to see in the world' or 'an eye for an eye only ends up making the whole world blind'.

I see this as some of poetry's power—to touch and move us more deeply than other types of writing or words; to even help us taste and sense the divine energy that inspires and guides all great peace builders of faith like Gandhi and his students: Martin Luther King Jr and Cesar Chavez of the United States; Desmond Tutu and Nelson Mandela of South Africa, to name a few.

I have taught Gandhi's teachings and his example of nonviolent resistance for many years to students of peace building from many countries, but during my last visit to India when I had the pleasure of meeting Santosh Bakaya and speaking on the Ethics of Conflict Resolution at the Institute for Advanced Studies, Winter School on Gandhi as well as at the Rajasthan University, and at an international conference on the nonviolent movements, did I learn how much more I have to learn about Gandhi's life, teachings and writings.

These poems will be a joyous means of doing so. The insight I received during my 2012 sabbatical in India brought compassion and empathy for Gandhi. I have often reflected that some of the world's greatest souls, minds, personalities and leaders have suffered greatly. Gandhi was assassinated after India's partition into 'Muslim Pakistan' and 'Hindu India' (India and Pakistan share the second world home for Muslims after Indonesia). Heartbroken and feeling deep grief over the resultant tragic slaughter of so many Muslims, Hindus and Sikhs, I imagine he died feeling a failure after spending a lifetime trying to model and encourage peace between Muslims and Hindus. He may have never even called himself a peace builder.

I will persist, however, in calling him the greatest peace builder the world has ever seen—not through the lens of earthly success or fulfillment of his hopes and aspirations, but because his spirit and teachings transcended Hindu-Muslim and many other divides; most importantly, his life. They continue to inspire and move people of many different ages, faiths and circumstances to stand against injustice and stand for the moral best of which human beings are capable.

Desmond Tutu, the archbishop of South Africa who rallied the world's religious leaders and communities against South Africa's apartheid, and became famous for calling South Africans post-apartheid to truth and reconciliation, is undeniably Christian. He is just one example who says something like the following: 'We do scant justice and honor to our God if we want, for instance, to deny that Mahatma Gandhi was a truly great soul, a holy man who walked closely with God. Our God would be too small if he was not also the God of Gandhi' (Tutu, 2011 p7). Reverend Tutu goes on, as Gandhi did, to appeal to all people of faith around the world (Muslim, Christian, Sikh, Hindu, Jewish, Buddhist…) that '(w) here there is injustice and oppression, where people are treated as if they were less than who they are—those created in the image of God—(people of faith) have no choice but to oppose, and oppose vehemently… that injustice and oppression' (Tutu, 2011, p19).

As a woman scholar and professor, I hope author Bakaya will appreciate my reasons for acknowledging that I do not write this foreword blind to the feminist scrutiny of Gandhi's relationships with women, just as I am not unaware of the critique of Martin Luther King Jr's relationships with women. Gandhi himself critiqued his early arrogance and misuse of authority with his wife. I do not see either of these fighters for justice and freedom as perfect human beings. I do not believe, however, that the world can afford to simply critique, disregard and discard such living examples of peace builders. We desperately need their examples and teachings. No one can deny that despite their limitations and human weaknesses, they were both exceptional human beings. As a feminist scholar, I invite all readers to be open to absolute truth as I believe Gandhi would have wanted, so that we can learn from their mistakes and encourage even greater exceptionality during these dark materialist competitive and too often, hate-filled times.

During my months of sabbatical in India, I spoke to and studied with some of Gandhi's most devoted students and disciples today. While Gandhi passionately sought to reconcile Muslims, Hindus and others throughout India, there are occasions when he went to Hindus first. While historians will likely never know whether such small details would have made critical difference, the history of peace building shows that impeccable impartiality to all concerned in a particular conflict may be necessary to build trust and move forward, especially when the mediator between conflicting parties is identified more with one of the parties than others.

While Gandhi famously announced he loved Christ, most of the world sees him as a Hindu. Nelson Mandela was a living example of such impeccable impartiality, or equal treatment of all concerned with a conflict, when he left his prison of twenty-seven years in South Africa and spoke for democracy, stating that the majority of South Africans, Black and White, recognised that apartheid had no future. Gandhi, too, had many such inspirational moments—as when he asked a warring Hindu to raise a Muslim child, orphaned in the violence, as a Muslim.

Gandhi aspired to purity. I have no doubt that if we could talk today, he would agree that he would have aspired to consistent impartiality with Muslims, Hindus and others if it would have united India for its future and avoided the tragic violence of partition. I stress the importance of 'impeccable and impartial' impartiality because today, unless a people see their leaders treating them as well as they treat others, democracy is not sustainable. A democratically elected leader is not enough. The recent popular ousting of the Muslim Brotherhood president of Egypt is a potent example. All those served by an alleged democracy must experience the devotion of their public servants; not see them preferring one group over another.

In the toughest of conflicts, leaders must be moral inspirations—like Gandhi, inspiring the best of their societies rather than petty interests. In the US, both King Jr and President Lincoln have played these rare and noble roles, transcending ordinary human reactiveness in destructive times and finding their ways to ultimately transform destructive human systems; in short, like Gandhi, against all odds. These lives deserve close study by all generations in the hope that similar exceptional beings and leaders can be nurtured and created to once again strategically challenge and prevail in the face of destructive life-harming elements and dynamics.

Gandhi's legacy (example and teachings) live on around the world today. It is seen in the Arab Spring and several other transitions from authoritarian and abusive regimes. A 2005 Freedom House Study examined sixty-seven such political transitions in recent decades. Nonviolent civic resistance was a driving force in fifty transformations. The stronger the nonviolent civic community, the deeper the transformation to democracy. Community organising and alliance building across difference of class, gender, belief, culture… that occurs with the best of nonviolent civic resistance and is also important for multicultural (religious…) democracy building (Chenoweth and

Stephan, 2012). It is likewise seen in my interdisciplinary field of negotiation, conflict resolution and peace building (hereinafter 'NCRP'), in a variety of popular conflict processes and research—not surprising, given Gandhi himself is quoted as saying, 'My joy was boundless. I had learned the true practice of law. I had learnt to find out the better side of human nature and to enter men's hearts. I realised the true function of a lawyer was to unite parties riven asunder… I lost nothing thereby—not even money; certainly not my soul' (writing on Gandhi in 1962). Gandhi's influence appears to have helped shape contemporary NCRP. In fact, with serious study, I find his influence permeating the teaching and practice of integrative negotiation and facilitative mediation at their best. They stress the importance of empowering self-determination for all and balancing power between the least and most powerful.

Gandhi also said 'my life is my message'. Such moral congruence, or walking one's talk, is essential to NCRP's building and deepening of trust as well as leadership influence and persuasion. Both Gandhi and NCRP further promote unconditional regard for all people, including suspension of judgment. This is expressed in Gandhi's words as 'hate the sin and not the sinner' or Harvard's Roger Fisher's words of 'separating people from the problem'. Both go on to advocate challenging injustice with love, or in contemporary negotiation research language 'generous tit for tat' and astute reframing of hostility to insightfully identify and respond to the most important underlying human need.

While so potent a pragmatist with grassroots strategy that succeeded again and again against all odds, Gandhi did not see himself as solely a political leader. He saw his life and efforts as spiritual and described listening for his 'still inner voice' as well as being aware of a constant witness. My students, especially the youngest, appear to share his hunger for truth. They ask to be taught how to 'be peace' rather than simply build peace.

As American scholar David Cortright (2009) said, '(My) inquiry into nonviolent social change turned into a quest for truth and the meaning of life'. Renowned American psychologist Abraham Maslow (1976) too said: 'If we want to know the possibilities for spiritual growth, value growth or moral development in human beings, then I maintain, we can learn the most by studying our most moral, ethical or saintly people.'

I would like to join many in advocating that Gandhi is one of these people and this poetic biography deserves close reading.

Maslow went on to assert that societies must nurture and prioritise the conditions that inspire and support such greatness and full potential. Both Gandhi's life and the field of NCRP give us some indications of what these broader societal conditions must be. Gandhi transcended ordinary human limitations again and again. The research informing NCRP refers to some of these limitations as overly simplistic dichotomies: us versus them; right versus wrong; women versus men... In Gandhi's words, 'in fighting the imagined enemy without, (we) neglect the enemy within'. What is called for in an extraordinary life and society is embracing and integrating life's rich complexities in inclusive ways, creating larger superordinate wholes, transforming apathy, and, most importantly, humanising the dehumanised oppressed through the transformative power of human encounter.

NCRP also teaches and promotes what is called reflective practice with action theory, informing and guiding the most effective of practice in the real world. The reader might ask why would anyone in the contemporary world be inspired to choose Gandhi's example and strategy of public service and truth-seeking over personal and material gain? NCRP research and modern examples offer answers to this question as well.

Research on what is called 'groupthink' shows that the worst and most tragic of decisions have been made when truth is abandoned for conformity with dominant norms. The US invasion of Iraq and failure to find 'weapons of mass destruction' is one example. Gandhi, in contrast, not only emulated masterful reflective practice on nonviolent resistance but also sustainable living and empowered self-reliance. These teachings have received relatively less attention and deserve study during times of global warming and warning.

The youngest of Silicon Valley millionaires might lead the way, particularly those retiring early and devoting themselves and their wealth to social entrepreneurship. I wish those who truly emulate Gandhi like Anṇa Hazare could join us at international forums to discuss what is the optimal modern balance between expert and authoritative strength and informed engaged citizenry.

Would Gandhi have praised Egypt's military when it supported mass nonviolent resistance? India's judicial system when it stood for justice on behalf of rape victims in the face of corrupt and non-responsive police? I would like to think so. Gandhi courageously stood for including and responding to the poorest and most vulnerable among us. Without such power balancing and compassion, our respective and proclaimed democracies will continue to deteriorate into mere havens for elites. Does the world truly need more? Our children, the youngest of our world, truly deserve more—principled democracies that 'walk their talk', transform apathy and inspire like Gandhi did.

I will close with Gandhi's famous words, 'When I despair, I remember that through history the way of truth and love has always won. There have been tyrants and murderers and for a time they seem invincible but in the end they always fall—think of it—always'.

—Nancy Diane Erbe, JD; LL M Professor
Member Review Committee
Fulbright Specialists Program
Negotiation, Conflict Resolution & Peacebuilding Program
California State University,
United States
12 November 2014

I want world
sympathy in
this battle of
Right against
Might.
Dandi M.K.Gandhi
5.4.'30

The Saga of a Sage

— Foreword by Tushar A Gandhi

Great grandson of Mahatma Gandhi

Of Porbandar and Rajkot
Of London and law court
Of a night at Petermaritzburg
To the jail in Johannesburg
Of tending to the wounded at Spionkop
And caring for the wounded Zulus in Kwazulu Natal
Of Phoenix and Tolstoy Farm
Of Satyagraha and life on a farm
Of Bramhacharya and also Kasturba
Of marriage at 13 a journey of a lifetime
Of making her clean night soil and sending her to jail
A life time of teaching her and learning too
Their unity endearing, their bond inspiring.

Of the return to his homeland
Triumphant from a distant land
The discovery of his motherland
Satyagraha in Kheda and Champaran

Of noncooperation and swadeshi too
Retreat in Chauri Chaura on principles
Confessing to sedition with pride and conviction
The March to Dandi with determination
A fistful of salt and steel in his heart
A voyage to the King's Round Table he went
On bended knees and an iron resolve.

And then he said Quit India
Now we must Do or Die he called
For freedom we fight without sword or spite
But stop we won't till the last left standing
Then his land did get freedom
But a price too dear in blood was paid
The land torn asunder its hearts filled with hate
And against the mobs on rampage
Walked the One-man Peace Force
With his tears he washed the blood and the hate
With grief in his heart he mourned his fate.

In the hour of his triumph
To walk alone was his fate
And then the bullets found his chest
With the name of his maker
Ram, R...a...m, R....a...m he left
With his last breath and blood
He quelled the fire of hate.
And then he was gone
The eternal into eternity.
Of this life of Mohan
His life his message
Of such a one as he
Who people would scarce believe
Had walked in flesh and blood
Once upon this earth
Tells Santosh in her verses
The life of Mohan
The saga of a Mahatma.

Author's Note

It was the afternoon of 13 August 1947, only two days before India's Independence. An old, exhausted and shattered ruin of a man was heading towards a building, another ruin, in a pre-war Chevrolet, itself ramshackle.

The cacophonous chorus of a clamorous crowd fell into his tired ears, *Traitor to the Hindus. Save Hindus, not Muslims*. The Chevrolet stopped, hailed by a shower of bottles and stones.

The youth howled full-throttled, the car door slowly opened.

The old, exhausted and shattered figure materialised on the scene. Lines from Tagore's famous song probably rang in his ears:

Trample the Thorns under Thy Tread
And Along the Blood Lined Track Travel Alone.

Fearlessly, the haggard but intrepid figure walked into the incensed crowd, braving the stony shower—alone, all alone. In the corridors of his brain, anguish simmered and emotions frothed.

The crowd was rooted to the spot. The frail figure and his followers moved towards Hydari House which stood on the edge of a canal in the predominantly Hindu Beliaghat district. The Muslim slum of Mianbagan, recently plundered by the Hindu youth, lay beyond the canal with its Doric pillars and carved balustrades. Hydari House was now merely a ghost of its former grandeur—a rotting ruin.

Was this frail man also a mere ghost of his former grandeur, a mere husk—hollow and hopelessly helpless—an icon who had outlived his use? A foolish old man who loved to dream and live in a fool's paradise?

Here, in this dark and decaying ruin owned by a Muslim, the miracle worker, in his last symbolic gesture hoped to construct a strong edifice of communal harmony—yearning to resurrect his dreams from the clutches of hate-ravaged humanity. Religious fanaticism held sway. Malevolence, mistrust and mayhem were in the air.

He had arrived in Calcutta on 9 August 1947 and promised to stay longer only if HS Suhrawardy, the former Prime Minister of Bengal, the man widely believed to be responsible for the Direct Action Day of 16 August 1946, accompanied him. Suhrawardy was expected to go with him to the building but he was late, so Gandhi went all alone.

'Why have you come here?' The crowd jeered.

'I have come here to serve Hindus and Muslims alike… you are welcome to turn against me if you wish; I have nearly reached the end of life's journey. I have not much further to go. But if you again go mad, I will not be a living witness to it.'

The magician in loin cloth had no magic wand, no magical hat to pull out rabbits from, not even a rabble-rousing voice, but only a heart full of love. He was chanting magical words. A hush fell on the crowd, the miracle man was at work, and his soft voice shook with moral fervour as he spoke.

'How can I, who am a Hindu by birth, a Hindu by creed and a Hindu of Hindus in my way of living, be an enemy of Hindus?'

It was this soft, feathery voice that had shaken many a comatose conscience, jerked many from a chronic slumber, shamed many into guilt. It was this indignant voice that had lashed out at the heavily bejeweled princes sitting on the dais at the inauguration ceremony of the Banaras Hindu University in Varanasi in 1916, exhorting them to strip themselves of their jewels.

He was forever evolving, trying to be the change he wanted to see around himself. He was not a man with an impressive musculature, or stunning looks, only a deceptively weak-looking human being with an exemplary moral strength, who could flex his moral muscles, bringing about an incredible metamorphosis in many a man bursting at the seams with belligerence—a strength which he acquired by self-introspection, self discipline, self-analysis and a rigid self-mastery.

On 29 August 1931, he had sailed from Bombay by the SS Rajputana as the sole delegate of the Indian National Congress, to attend the Second Round Table Conference to decide the fate of India, which was being held in London. He disembarked at the French sea port of Marseilles in order to catch the train to London. The French customs officer on duty asked him whether he had anything to declare. He had promptly replied: 'I am a poor mendicant. My kit consists of two spinning wheels, a few jail utensils, a can of goat's milk, four loin cloths, two towels—and my reputation which cannot be worth much.' No sartorial accoutrements of immaculately designed suits for this poor mendicant in his weird attire, and meagre possessions, but during the course of his life he had acquired so formidable a reputation, that during the Dandi March, his passive defiance of making salt had shaken the British empire.

In the strife-torn world, this half-naked figure went around spreading love like a salve, giving the healing touch with his calloused hands, tossing away the brickbats that came his way, kicking away the stumbling blocks that obstructed his path, closing his ears to the jeers and sneers, winning the hearts of people on the way.

'What a spellbinder this old man is', remarked one.

'No matter how heavy the odds—he doesn't know defeat', seconded another when he tried to woo the angry youth during his stay in Hydari House.

In a last symbolic move, he had played his master stroke. If Suhrawardy and he could stay together under one roof, why not everyone else?

He had won over the warring youth with his indefatigable efforts—the peace warrior had won yet another victory, well-armed with a love-laced armoury.

His weapon of nonviolence was a potent weapon which wreaked havoc, unleashed a wave of fear in the British, making them rethink their perception about the half-naked figure in whose charismatic presence even fully-clad people appeared jarringly naked—fully exposed before the world with their flaws and shortcomings.

The boy who had been afraid of snakes, ghosts and demons

as a child, had fearlessly followed what he thought was the right path, becoming a beacon light for a beleaguered humanity, making many like Martin Luther King Jr, Nelson Mandela, Aung San Suu Kyi mention how he had a great influence on their thought processes.

There is violence on the streets, every nook and cranny erupting in violence at the least provocation, violence in minds, violence in hearts, violence in general elections, violence in student elections, violence in utterances—violence seems to have become a creed which everyone seems to be following, both in overt and covert ways. There are victims of heard violence, there are victims of unheard of violence. The entire world seems to have been reduced to a war zone where dissenting voices are throttled, and voices speaking for dignity are silenced by the gun. There are so many instances of mobs setting fire to shops and offices, vehicles and houses. There is violence over water, violence over loud music, violence over posts in social networking sites, violence over violence.

The enchanting music of love tends to get drowned in the strident and ear-callusing cries of venomous hatred. We do not seem to realise that every act of violence diminishes us, reduces us. Without the sublimity of love, we are stunted pygmies, groping in the dark.

Many of my students crinkle their noses at the mention of Gandhi; they think that he has lost his relevance—but my questions to them are—can nonviolence ever lose its relevance, can peace ever be a thing of the past, can love and forgiveness ever be anachronistic? Gandhi stood for all these. Hence he continues to be relevant today—no matter what the detractors say.

Agreed, he had some shortcomings—but who doesn't? He was, after all, an imperfect human being, who candidly talked about his weaknesses, his whole life a series of experiments through which he tried to better himself.

Let his detractors criticise him, let them lampoon him, let them heap venom at him for his shortcomings—but let them not miss the wood for the trees.

Let them realise the magnanimity the wood has to offer, let them feel the fresh, invigorating breeze of love, harmony and forgiveness wafting across the wood. Let them be lost in the benevolent charm of the wood.

A man, who locked horns with Smuts; nauseated the refined sensibilities of Winston Churchill who equated his form of politics with chicanery (as an out-of-work politician in the 1930s, Churchill said, 'Gandhism and all it stands for will sooner or later, have to be grappled with and finally crushed'. In1943, when he went on fast, Churchill hoped that the fast would prove fatal for him. When he was imprisoned and later released in 1944, and corresponded with the Viceroy of India about a timetable for the British withdrawal from India, Churchill called him 'a traitor who ought to be put back in prison'); inspired respect in judge Broomfield, filled King George V with wrath, lambasted Kasturba, his better half; negotiated and parleyed on equal terms with Lord Irwin, much to the chagrin of Churchill; beguiled people with his toothless charm, awed them with his multi-dimensionality, surprised them with his fantastically resilient spirit which had the potential to pick up the debris of shattered dreams and rebuild new dreams, at times raising the hackles of even those close to him, making them wonder at his naivete! But that was Gandhi, complete with his fads, foibles, idiosyncrasies, whims and fancies. And his wicked sense of humour.

He had no dearth of detractors, even those who were close to him, often made fun of many of his whimsicalities. Sarojini Naidu, one of his greatest supporters, is said to have quipped with her typical sardonic humour, 'it costs a lot of money to keep Gandhiji in poverty'.

On one occasion, Churchill is said to have told Smuts, 'you are responsible for our troubles in India—you had Gandhi for years and did not do away with him'. Smuts is said to have replied, 'when I put him in prison—three times—all Gandhi did was to make a pair of bedroom slippers'.

He was not a saint but a human being, who never said that he was perfect, one who candidly wrote about his indiscretions. How otherwise would we have known about them, had he not written about them?

This nurse, washer man, gardener, champion spinner, jailbird, bibliophile had carved a monumentally extraordinary life out of the ordinary circumstances he had been born into.

He struck many lifelong friendships with people like Christian missionary Charlie F Andrews, who had given all his money to the South African movement, and who he affectionately called Christ's Faithful Apostle, based on his initials—CFA. Armed with a persuasive intellect and a rare moral rectitude, he had come to South Africa on Gokhale's persuasion and was immediately struck by Gandhi's knowledge of Christian values. Although theirs was a mutual admiration society, they disagreed on many a subject. East Prussian Jewish architect Hermann Kallenbach was so influenced by Gandhi's views on satyagraha that he donated his 1,100 acre farm near Johannesburg, where Tolstoy Farm was set up, which became a perfect example of a spartan life style, social equality and self-sustained economy, where the twosome even enjoyed bicycle rides. (Gandhi could not meet him for twenty-three years, after he left him behind in Johannessburg.)

Although bonded together by a common utopianism, the sage of Shantiniketan Rabindranath Tagore and the half-naked figure did not see eye-to-eye on many issues; Tagore wondering how the charka could bring about a revolution in India, and how the Bihar earthquake could be the comeuppance for the peoples' belief in the evil of untouchability.

Copiously caricatured, cruelly criticised, laughingly lampooned, sneeringly satirised and deferentially deified, Gandhi strongly believed 'that if you approached people with trust and affection, you would have ten-fold trust and thousand-fold affection returned to you'.

Under the deft handling of this visionary, khadi, salt and charkha gained an iconic symbolism, the poor, downtrodden, the marginalised identifying with these at every step. Under his leadership, the comatose people rose in 'unvanquishable number', 'like lions after slumber' and shook away their emasculating chains, their 'man-forged manacles', their servile mindsets, and their low self-esteem.

I would like to sign off with a word to the youth: Let us remember that he was an ordinary human being, who created a niche for himself with his extraordinariness, let us not put the halo of divinity around him, let us not sing paeans for him, and let us accept him with all his flaws and blemishes—for was not he a common man with the common failings that every commoner is prone to—yet, a common man who left behind an uncommon legacy.

In the present strife-torn world, where love, forgiveness, selflessness are in a pathetic short supply, Gandhi's words need to be followed, as opposed to the stridently menacing tones of vitriol and the insidious currents of hatred we appear to be surrounded with at every turn of life.

In the crosscurrents of hatred, let us prick up our ears and allow ourselves the luxury of listening to his powerful words: An eye for an eye and a tooth for a tooth will make the whole world blind.

Let us not yearn for this blindness.

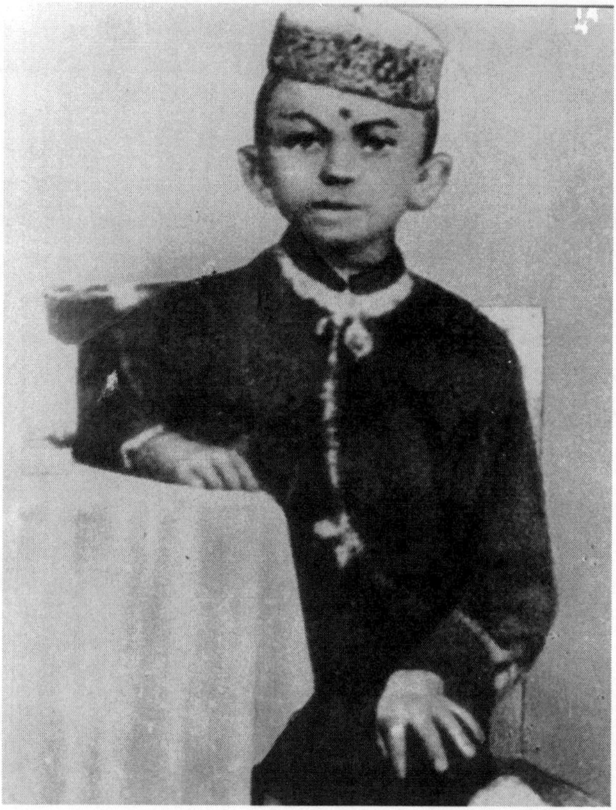

Gandhi as a schoolboy

A Star is Born

On 2nd October 1869, this magician took birth.
Whose nicknames would soon spread on earth.
Sarojini's fancy this Mickey Mouse tickled
While the imperialists their noses crinkled.
Churchill called him a half-naked fakir in mirth.

Karam Chand, Dewan to the sovereign of the land
At home, this father ruled with an iron hand.
His mother, so devout
Putlibai no doubt
Gave birth to and inspired his firm moral stand.

In Porbandar, he went to an elementary school.
The tables remained unmastered though no fool.
At age seven, to Rajkot his family shifted.
Though not extraordinarily gifted
He passed primary and later high school.

The inspector of schools set a spelling test.
He misspelt kettle, the teacher tried his best
To make him cheat
He rejected this deceit
The truth was not to be toyed with, even in jest!

Legend of Harishchandra put his dream in motion
And the myth of Shravana's parental devotion.
These heroes stole
Deep into his soul
Carrying his heart away as though upon the ocean.

At thirteen, his early marriage came
To Kasturba, whose age was the same.
In this conjugal bond
He grew very fond
Of his simple mate, who now shared his name.

In school he shunned football, gymnastics, exercise.
Vexed when his teacher accused him of lies
When he failed to be on time
Mendacity was not his crime
At this accusation, his wrath he could not disguise.

He had been nursing his father who was ill
So with indignation his heart did fill.
Utterly humiliated
His teeth he grated
But swallowed this accusatory bitter pill.

Unscrupulously Sheikh Mahtab cast his spell
Mohan stormed into this friendship pell-mell.
His daring and athletic build
Had him with awe filled
On non-vegetarianism, his mind started to dwell.

Of ghosts, thieves and snakes, Mohan was scared.
But in Mehtab's company, many forbidden things dared.
This proved disastrous
For the boy veracious
So he gave him up, as for his family he cared.

Smoking a transgression, meat-eating another yet
Stealing a bit of gold from his brother's armlet.
A written confession followed this theft
Forgiving him his ailing father wept
As he had stolen to clear his brother's debt.

He lost his father and later passed matriculation.
Now what to study by way of higher education
Was the question
Which in the family created tension.
But a friendly suggestion filled him with elation.

Mavji Dave, a family friend, offered advice
To study law in England, Mohan didn't think twice.
His brother worried about the fare
While he built castles in the air
His mother her displeasure could not disguise.

Gandhi with his brother

If he vowed not to touch women, meat and wine
He could go, he was told, now he felt fine.
But still anxious was his mother
The fare was arranged by his brother
After the initial fear, he floated on cloud nine.

Young and Unsure

In September 1888, he sailed for Southampton
Threatened by his caste with excommunication
As crossing the ocean
It considered pollution
This eighteen-year-old defied humiliation.

Majumdar offered to share his cabin on the trip.
The gawky teenager didn't want the offer to slip.
Filled with nervous elation
He jumped at this invitation
And reveled in this friendship on the ship.

The Junagarh lawyer was mature and wise
Joy at his amiability Mohan could not disguise.
The gangling youth
Was quite uncouth
About the lurking dangers he couldn't surmise.

Gandhi with wife Kasturba

With awe, the vast sea he contemplated
By card players, musical instruments fascinated.
The dining room
For him spelled doom
The bantering of the English folk he hated.

In unfamiliar ambience he was trapped at sea
In a cocoon of silence, sailing perpetually.
Its surreal quality
Filled him with perplexity
The boy had no choice but right there to be.

Mustering courage, with the English he drank tea
Who wondered who this person could be.
Some made the demand
Put a fork in his hand
When coaxed into eating meat, he wanted to flee.

With nervousness Mohan's skin tingled
On this voyage the teenager hardly mingled.
Bogged down by taciturnity
He lost every opportunity
To talk to those Majumdar singled.

Majumdar asked him to be talkative and bold
In environment formidable, his blood ran cold.
Like a vulnerable kid
In the cabin he hid
Not daring to do what by Majumdar he was told.

Repelled by the non-vegetarian food that some ate
He felt homesick and his misery was great.
But filled with gratitude
When a problem of great magnitude
Was solved by Majumdar, his amiable ship mate.

He charmed an attendant into cooking Indian food.
This was no fad or whimsical turn of mood.
Mohan felt he would smother
If he betrayed his mother
And the portents would definitely be skewed.

Frantically throbbed his heart at this voyage maiden.
After a few days, the ship anchored at Aden.
By Majumdar accompanied
He did not feel weak-kneed
Touring for an hour in a carriage lightly laden.

Awestruck by many a resplendent sight
The Suez Canal overwhelmed him with delight.
Fascinated by the visual treat
But tortured by the heat
Dashing to the top for a whiff of air in the night.

He found Port Said a seat of many a frill.
Charged for listening to music angered him still.
He parted with pennies six
Putting him in a fix
The frugal boy had little money in his till.

Sans family he reached the centre of civilization.
Was his dream of seeing England an infatuation?
He missed his mother and wife
But wasn't this the life
After which he had hankered with high expectation?

Caught between the devil and the deep blue sea
He yearned for the way things used to be.
'Hold on' said his inner voice
So, the young lad had no choice
But to stay and adjust to this outlandish country.

On a Saturday he went ashore in flannels white
A dress he naively thought was right.
But he was shocked
When by the Southampton folks mocked
For his attire being such a fright.

In matters of English etiquette he was raw.
So this he cultivated, with his study of law.
With a new vigour
This lanky figure
Learned English manners to camouflage this flaw.

A chimney-pot hat, a double-watch chain of gold
A tie and a Bond Street suit made him bold.
With a new-found passion
He parted his hair in the right fashion
To the idea of becoming an Englishman, sold.

His home and country he continued to miss
Yearning to lose the label of the naïve novice
He cultivated social graces
Wearing many masks and faces
In trying to be polished, he found no bliss.

He took lessons in dancing, French, elocution.
For character development, no substitution.
So he gave up superficiality,
And a false sense of propriety
And turned to simple living as the true solution.

Home, Sweet Home

Leaving England after nearly three years of time
The barrister-at-law sailed home to India's sweet clime.
His heart sang
His ears rang
With melodious sounds of his motherland sublime.

In Bombay he felt things would never be the same.
Burned by destiny's cruel flame
A bolt from the blue
Shattered everything held true.
His mother had died, an orphan he became.

The shock wreaked havoc with his equanimity
Threatening to destroy his tranquility.
Yet checking his tears
And quelling his fears
Mohan bore this loss with exemplary dignity.

Gandhi as a young barrister in 1891-92

The storm about his trip raged within his caste
A faction readmitted him, trying to heal the past.
But he felt bad
And also sad
To be treated so unkindly left him aghast.

He condemned rituals and caste bigotry
On his brother's insistence giving into tyranny.
Caste ties he couldn't sever
So, in Nasik's sacred river
He reluctantly took a dip purificatory.

In Rajkot his brother gave a caste dinner
Mohan seethed, feeling he was no sinner.
Yet in deference to his brother's desire
He agreed to soothe the ire
Of the caste-gods, emerging a winner!

The advice of some friends he heeded
And to the metropolis Bombay, he proceeded.
To study Indian law
In which he was pretty raw
To gain experience in the courts much needed.

Pherozashah Mehta's legal acumen, mind-boggling
Badruddin Tyabji's aura awe-inspiring.
This, by a friend he was told
Which failed to make him bold.
The information was for him nerve-racking.

His moral uprightness proved to be a liability
He found that he had no legal ability.
He twiddled his thumbs
Waiting for legal crumbs
Dozing in the High Court, ruing his incapability.

His Bombay sojourn turned into a disaster
Mohan remained but a brief-less barrister.
He failed to make a go
So felt absolutely low
Sans money, sans cases, lost was this character.

After a disaster in the Small Causes Court
He felt he could no longer hold the fort.
So, in less than a year
He was back shedding many a tear
From where he had started in Rajkot.

Setting up his office, moderately he earned
Drafting pleas for the poor, a lesson he learned
That earning such a pittance
Made absolutely no sense
For better compensation now Gandhi yearned.

In the state of Kathiawar, corruption held sway.
To disrupt the atmosphere, came a hopeful ray.
An offer so tempting
Unhappiness preempting
Promising to save him from dismay.

To Protean Lands

With an unnamed passion, he was burning
When, in his favour the tide began turning.
A Kathiawar firm
For a one-year term
Sent him to South Africa, answering his yearning.

They offered 105 pounds and a return fare
In which he found an opportunity rare
To see a country new
This time his doubts were few
As traveling was no longer an unusual affair.

Leaving Kasturba would mean pang of separation.
He was nonetheless filled with grateful elation.
He asked her not to fear
As he would be gone only for a year.
Now he braced himself for the migration.

Gandhi, with his associates in South Africa 1894-95

This barrister was the most outraged on earth
When the agent couldn't get him first class berth.
Doubting the agent's truth
And considering it uncouth
To travel second class, vowed to secure his worth.

When confronted, the ship's chief officer made note
Of his turban and mismatching frock coat.
He offered a place
Within his own cabin space
Reaching Lamu, after thirteen days on the boat.

At this port, for three hours, they went ashore.
For sightseeing and the new land to explore.
After a near mishap
Which his energy did sap
They were back in the ship, now no longer sore.

Mombasa was the next port, followed by Zanzibar
Halting for a while near a luxuriant sandbar.
They were there eight days or ten
Before moving on again
They still had to journey very far.

Towards the end of May, they reached Durban
Mohan attired in his outlandish coat and turban.
He aroused curiosity
But carried himself with dignity
Though hurt by the snobbishness he found a burden.

In a Durban court, a magistrate commanded
'Remove your turban', prejudice demanded.
He point blank refused.
The magistrate felt abused.
Gandhi wrote of this discrimination underhanded.

Soon this unwelcome visitor gained certain notoriety
Some upheld his claim, others shunned his society
But the man turban-clad
Unafraid to take a stand
In defense of his customs that held no impropriety.

The train reached Maritzburg in the evening late.
Nothing unusual but again intervened fate.
A White man boarded the train
Who came under great strain
On seeing that a coloured man was to be his mate.

A constable came to push him out of the carriage.
Leaving him on the platform, bag and baggage.
He was in a sorry plight
On the bitterly cold night
The railway authorities took charge of his luggage!

He sat in the waiting room, gripped by confusion
If he kept quiet would he be guilty of collusion?
For his rights, should he fight?
Use his entire main and might
Or return to India after his work's conclusion?

These were thoughts that racked his brain
Placing him under great emotional and mental strain
Should he seek redress
And suffer more in the process?
He now bought a ticket to Pretoria on the next train.

He reached Charlestown, where he intended to ride
By coach to Standerton, but there were Europeans inside.
He was rejected rudely
With the driver he sat, moodily.
Asked to mount the footboard, human rights denied.

Mohan stared down the officer, whose eyes were cold.
For his seat in the train, insisted the 24-year-old.
The Maritzburg incident
In his heart made a dent
These blows to his self-respect made him bold.

The White official could not bear this impertinence.
He beat him, seething with racial arrogance.
A quiet human dignity
Confronted racial brutality
Bravely he faced this test of endurance.

If he was coloured, where was his fault?
Some White passengers protested this cowardly assault.
But he did not retaliate
Violence he did hate
The conductor stopped, threatening a fresh assault.

The train reached Standerton after dark
The episode had left an indelible mark.
He had learnt to say no
To both friend and foe
Now on a new journey he was about to embark.

Next morning he proceeded to Johannesburg city.
His heart not actually singing a happy ditty.
For the Standerton episode
Was a heavy load
Making him fume at the conductor's audacity!

'Don't worry', with soothing words he was consoled.
'Learn to pocket the insults', at Standerton told.
Johannesburg he reached at night
Into a cab hurling his frame slight
He headed for Grand National Hotel, quite bold!

The manager apologised in a tone polite.
When Gandhi asked for a room that night.
His mind a tumult
At yet another insult
Resolving to do something, for his countrymen's plight!

This London-qualified barrister on first assignment
Got a ticket for Pretoria in first class compartment.
'What do you mean by troubling the gentleman?'
Protested his co-passenger, an Englishman
Restraining his eviction from the compartment!

Gandhi with Indian community leaders in South Africa

The guard called him a coolie and grumbled
While the train with ominous sounds rumbled.
He fumed at the derogatory label
The Englishman said, 'Make yourself comfortable'.
With his feelings of indignation he now fumbled.

Gandhi with supporters and friends leading movement against Natal law

Centrestage

In his heart injustice turned like a knife
He called a meeting that'd begin his public life.
He spoke with maturity
Exhorting his community
To reclaim dignity without resorting to strife.

Rigour heaped upon rigour filled his fragile figure
With a new enthusiasm and vigour
His faith infectious
Made him courageous
Passionately he strove for a role bigger.

The meek youth was now a leader of men
Who could preach, moralize and wield the pen!
To his client his first duty lay
Legal practice no child's play.
So he now tried to hone his legal acumen!

He drilled into the parties the futility of litigation
Succeeding in making them accept arbitration.
None felt nettled
Out of court the matter was settled
His mission achieved, sans guilt of instigation!

Back to Durban he went, to be home bound
A newspaper report turned his plans around.
What he read in the *Natal Mercury*
Filled his heart with great fury
His countrymen were being forced to the ground.

A Bill in Natal legislature aimed to disenfranchise
Indian settlers, in a way both unjust and unwise.
Its sinister implication
Filled him with mortification
Within him, he could feel a righteous anger rise.

Wailed his friends, 'we are unlettered and lame
And we do not understand their wily game'.
He listened in attention rapt
Couldn't think of an answer apt
Hamletian indecisiveness he vainly tried to tame.

'Stay for a month longer', they pleaded
He twisted and turned, aware he was needed.
They implored in one voice
Giving him no choice
Surely his plans wouldn't suffer if he conceded?

'This is the first nail in the coffin', he moaned
For a month his return he postponed.
And jumped into the fray
A silver lining in the clouds grey.
Now the Indians no longer groaned.

Fired with vigour, he got ready for the kill
Which meant in the assembly opposing the Bill.
Quickly they dispatched a petition
Which created an impression
But its passage couldn't be stopped. Task uphill!

On his shoulders now a great responsibility
Which opened in him the forces of maturity.
He urged the men to cast away slough
And onward vigourously plough
Fighting for their rights in a spirit of solidarity.

His guidance a boon to his community, unlettered.
The warrior set to work on another plea, undeterred
Which was to England sent
Not a minor accomplishment
The London Times supported these men, fettered.

The petition with 10,000 names caused curiosity.
Receiving the much-needed publicity.
Thus the brief-less pleader
Was now the unquestioned leader
Of the beleaguered Indian community.

To the centrestage thus was he pitch-forked
Which his hidden capabilities uncorked.
The timorous youth
Once so uncouth
With strength rare, at the injustice a snook cocked!

The month over, now followed a renewed importunity
Which he could not view with cold objectivity.
So again his stay he prolonged
And through a strategy multi-pronged
Into a fractured community injected unity.

In order to clean the all-round mess
He established the Natal Indian Congress.
With indefatigable capacity
He tried to build solidarity
In the Indian community which floundered clueless.

For him, legal practice became a minor occupation
More important things cried for concentration.
Spirits not sagging
And energy unflagging
He attended to problems all, with an undying passion.

A bleeding man, teeth broken, clothes tattered
Complained, by his master he'd been battered.
Bala Sundaram his name
Whose only claim to fame
Was that by a European he was battered.

For a certificate he sent him to a doctor in a rage
His entire body shaking at this blatant outrage.
Securing the certificate
He took him to a magistrate
Who summoned this employer savage.

About indentured labour he vigourously read the laws
Which he realised were teeming with flaws.
On he slogged, untired
A hope he inspired
In the labourers that he supported their cause.

With their problems, they poured day and night.
Needless to say, this filled him with delight.
He made a deep study of their condition
When on them was levied a 25-pound taxation
Now he campaigned to put this right.

The labourers were bogged down by resignation
But the Congress started an intense agitation.
The tax was reduced to pound three
No time for complacent glee
He was now filled with a new determination.

His aim was now its total abolition
Onwards he marched on this sincere mission.
With faith unflinching
Morale unflagging
His aim he chased with moral gumption.

Gandhi and his associates in a nursing brigade during the Boer War, 1899

Power of Pamphlets

In mid-1896, to India he went to get support
In South Africa his men held the fort.
After three years, no longer adrift
To South Africa his family he wanted to shift.
From Calcutta he travelled to Bombay, for Rajkot.

On the problems of Indian settlers he wrote a tract
In the Green Pamphlet presenting a pertinent fact.
Dispatching it to people influential
Which he thought would be beneficial
In convincing them that it was time to act.

Like a bolt the bubonic plague ravaged Bombay.
In Rajkot spread stark terror, cold and gray.
His services he volunteered
His strength he geared
To this new cause and entered the fray.

Followed a country-wide tour for public education
To the cause which was his moral obligation.
In Bombay, his meeting with the uncrowned king
Pherozeshah Mehta made his heart sing.
In awe he had held this man of great erudition.

Mehta listened to him in rapt attention.
'I must call a public meeting here', he did mention.
Under his patronage distinguished
This important task he accomplished.
Moments before the meeting, filled with tension.

The hall was filled with a restless audience
And when he stood up, he started feeling tense
His voice sank lower
With fear he did cower
His speech, read by Wacha, was heard in silence.

Sounds of 'shame, shame' rent the air
As they heard of the treatment unfair.
He was elated
That though belated
They had got an idea of the unjust affair.

After his Bombay sojourn, to Poona he went
On meeting Tilak and Gokhale bent.
Both filled him with delight
Overwhelming him with their might
Promising to help him to the fullest extent.

Bhandarkar, he met at their suggestion
His fatherly warmth filled him with jubilation.
At the meeting Bhandarkar presided
And Gandhi he selflessly guided
His heart danced at this unexpected reception.

Poona meeting gave him the boost much needed.
Now to Madras the happy man proceeded.
Making an impression profound
A sympathetic audience found
With great enthusiasm, his speech they heeded.

Like hot cakes, was the Green Pamphlet sold
Making him exuberant and bold
Still a long way to go
The boat he had to row
On the situation he was now getting a strong hold.

In Calcutta it was difficult, here none he knew.
SN Banerjee said that the problems were not few.
Saunders, editor of *The Englishman,*
He found to be a perfect gentleman
A lifelong friendship sprung up between the two.

Local leaders did not give him a warm reception
His brow lined, filling him with utter frustration.
But *The Statesman*
And *The Englishman*
For his devotion, were full of appreciation.

When a Calcutta meeting was afoot as a boon.
A cable came asking him to come to Durban soon.
He set off from homeland
In the ship Courland
With his family, unmindful of rain or typhoon.

For them a dress code he set with conviction.
Shoes cramped, stockings stank with perspiration.
There was no argument
And no resentment
As they knew unheeded would go any objection.

When four days from Natal, there was a gale
Which horrified both male and female.
Nature's fury mocked
The ship rolled and rocked
All thought it would soon capsize in the gale.

For one day, they grappled with the weather unfair
The storm ceased, the sun smiled a smile rare.
People beamed
Now it seemed
That the gale had only been a scary nightmare.

But of this storm Gandhi had little fear
Among the passengers he spread good cheer.
Had to swallow another draught
When in another storm was caught
Unaware was Gandhi of this turbulence so near.

For Durban, the same day had sailed, another ship.
In the Courland, Gandhi struck a warm friendship.
On 19th December, 1896 they cast anchor
Unaware of the rancor
That would be their lot. One more hardship!

He had become the target of an allegation
The Natal Whites had received condemnation
At his hands, so they fumed with rage
At this brazen outrage
Threatening to drown Gandhi for this vilification!

Righteously indignant and filled with gall
That he planned to flood Transvaal and Natal
With labourers unindentured
Into danger he had ventured
With 800 passengers on the ship—things were droll!

Twenty-three days, passengers were quarantined
For reasons of health, Whites weren't inclined
To let them disembark.
On a vindictive path they did embark.
The devious plans of Gandhi churned in their mind.

Gandhi had no doubts about his innocence
In support of which he had ample evidence.
Their unfounded rancour
Didn't fill him with anger
Amply convinced of the power of nonviolence.

The captain was told that Whites were outraged.
And against Gandhi, highly enraged.
Destiny played another hand
At dusk, he was asked to land.
Came the legal advisor, a new alternative emerged.

With Gandhi, Laughton, the adviser had a talk
Whose friend lived two miles from the dock.
So, this short route
They were asked to cover on foot
Gandhi agreed, bracing for a two-mile walk.

In a carriage were driven his children and wife.
Thankfully, there was no danger to anyone's life.
But he did not baulk
When he got another knock
Youngsters recognised him; danger was rife.

'Gandhi', they shouted in tones menacing.
Men rushed and joined in this shouting.
The crowd swelled
And they yelled
'Gandhi, Gandhi', stones and eggs pelting.

This fury Laughton's earlier optimism belied.
The stone-pelters were now a human tide.
He felt a fainting fit
When by more stones hit
Laughton was forcibly dragged from his side.

Front railings of a house he tried to catch
Alas, for the irate mob no match.
Then came a Good Samaritan
A parasol-carrying woman
Destiny another conspiracy trying to hatch?

While the crowd looked on in amazement
Mrs Alexander, wife of the police superintendent
The woman good
Came and stood
Between him and the crowd; brave accomplishment!

The crowd had now gone absolutely insane
Danger lurked everywhere, Gandhi was in pain.
Her parasol kept the stones at bay
On that day ominously gray
Befuddled was the crowd, the stone pelting in vain.

This quelled the wrath of the mob tumultuous
Thus escaped Gandhi from the situation perilous.
To his destination escorted
The problem not yet sorted
Destiny for him was laying plans venomous!

Rustomji's house was by yelling Whites surrounded
The superintendent's fears were not ill-founded.
Louder became the cries
Gandhi crept out in disguise
The crowd outside was raucous and confounded.

An Indian constable's uniform, scarf on his head
Disguised as the shrewd superintendent had said.
With detectives two
What else could Gandhi do
But follow what the wise cop had said?

By a by-lane they reached a neighbouring shop.
The plan of the cop was not a flop.
Negotiating the gunny bags in the godown
Without tripping or falling down
They groped on, and reached the gate of this shop.

To a carriage, they threaded their way.
This was definitely no child's play!
It took them to the police station
It was at this junction
Alexander broke the news; shrewdness at display.

That Gandhi had escaped, he shrewdly intoned.
At this news the crowd visibly groaned.
Some furiously angry
Refused to believe the story
Others not finding him inside, mourned.

Of the incident there was condemnation
Which was not a figment of the imagination.
This assault cowardly
Was very dastardly
Many wanted the culprits' prosecution.

Reluctant to book anyone his determination.
This was an example of his moral gumption.
That despite his humiliation
He did not want the culprits' prosecution.
The villain was *Reuter*'s mangled interpretation.

His refusal to prosecute created an impression
Adding to his practice, enhancing his reputation.
The Mahatma lying dormant
Was making his presence felt
He set up home, unswayed by adulation.

In a house in the suburbs the family stayed
Where Indian and European guests visits paid.
In vegetarianism he believed
For which many brickbats he received
For his household now greater plans he laid.

He craved to serve the wounded and sick
Which was not the whim of an eccentric.
His inherent compassion
Yearned to find expression
For two hours, in a hospital, he tended the sick.

This humanitarian work he did with care
Dressing the wounds of lepers, with kindness rare.
His watch-word became simplicity
Of funds there was no scarcity
Learning to starch collars and cut his own hair.

In the 1899 Boer War, he supported the Empire
With an army of 10,000 serving on the line of fire.
They faced many a hardship
But under Gandhi's leadership
Dauntless they moved, though the situation was dire.

Marching 25 miles a day, the wounded they carried.
On stretchers, with sincerity, not at all harried.
When the corps was disbanded
Their selfless service was applauded.
In 1901 after the war, no longer he tarried.

Call of the Motherland

On his return, with a new desire he burned.
To go back to his motherland, he yearned.
With a heavy heart he bid adieu
To old friends and new
Sailing at the end of 1901, with a lesson learned.

Having distanced himself from a life of pelf
On the horns of a dilemma he found himself.
On him parting gifts were bestowed
This he felt was a heavy load
Craving to shake away this guilt from his self.

With Kasturba followed a heated discussion
Who despaired of this husbandly persecution.
The gifts be returned he insisted
That temptations be resisted
At this, she shed tears in frustration.

Kasturba with four Gandhi children

She needed them for daughters-in-law she argued.
Unflinching he stood his ground, not being rude.
Consent was finally extorted
The dilemma was thus sorted
This decision to his dying day, he never rued.

Gifts received in 1896 and 1901, were returned
He believed, such gifts needed to be spurned.
He was morally intoxicated
Initially by Kasturba berated
Later, she appreciated the lesson jointly learned.

They were deposited after a trust-deed.
Thus, the load was lifted, a wise decision indeed.
He heaved a relieved sigh
The gifts in the bank would lie
To be withdrawn when the community felt a need.

In time to attend the Congress meet in Calcutta
Presided over by majestic orator Dinshaw Wacha.
He moved spending time
In his country's clime
To Calcutta, travelling with Phirozeshah Mehta.

Mehta agreed to admit his resolution
Did this mean a fulfillment of his expectation?
With Wacha and Setalvad there
He could not dare
To plead for something concrete in the session.

With fanfare, Dinshaw Wacha was taken to camp
To Ripon College, Gandhi went, spirits not damp.
But he was shocked
And all but gawked
At the insanitary condition in the volunteers' camp.

'It is the scavenger's work', told point blank
When he asked, why the premises stank.
The stink all-pervasive
He found oppressive
He asked for a broom, was he a crank?

A cleaning-up operation began this man energetic
Feeling the condition fit for an epidemic.
Aghast, the volunteers stared
At this man who bravely dared
To infuse some order in the situation chaotic!

For a month in Calcutta, as Gokhale's guest
Who insisted that he should try to get abreast
Of the affairs in the country
By using his time and energy
So, Gandhi ventured forth, facing the test.

He yearned to see the metropolitan city
Meet Justice Mitter living in the same locality.
To visit the Kali temple keen
It could not go unseen
But the genuflecting beggars were an audacity.

Opposed to alms for beggars physically fit
He was scandalised and his teeth he grit
When mendicants few
Able bodied beggars too
Beseeched for alms, not ashamed a bit.

The path to the temple was with supplicants filled.
Which in his mind myriad thoughts milled.
Not much later
He received a shock greater
Knowing that to propitiate Kali, goats were killed.

But doing anything was beyond his capacity.
He prayed that someone moved with divine pity
Might see their sorry plight
And set things right
Putting an end to this reprehensible atrocity.

Listening to Bengali music at a celebration
At Brabmo Samaj filled him with elation.
By Belur Math fascinated
His enthusiasm deflated
Vivekananda he couldn't meet as was his expectation.

Sister Nivedita's love for Hinduism he admired
Religious institutions he visited, not feeling tired.
Finding the Burmese women energetic
But the men lethargic
When to Burma he went, with zest fired.

The first Indian National Congress session meets in Bombay, 1885

Appalled at the condition of third class compartment
And inchoate with anger and disappointment
That it had become a spittoon
This he realised very soon
That by littering people were deriving enjoyment.

In Benaras, he found hypocrisy rampant
The greed of the custodians of religion unpleasant.
The Kashivishvanath temple unclean
And the pandas sly and mean.
Now followed his next visit to Annie Besant.

The World Beckons

After practicing in Rajkot, to Bombay he went
Where he prospered better, his spirits exuberant.
But destiny played another hand
Forcing him to leave his motherland
In response to a cable, from Durban sent.

Where he was to lead an Indian delegation
To the Secretary of State for colonies, Chamberlain.
Reaching at the time appointed
Gandhi was sorely disappointed
To find that he had no time for this deputation.

This humiliation could not his confidence shake
When told the permit was given to him by mistake.
He seethed at the impunity
Of retorting, not getting an opportunity
He pocketed the insult as much was at stake!

Gandhi and British India

By CLAIR PRICE

Mahatma Karamchand Gandhi.

The New York Times

INDIAN OPINION

Founded by ·MAHATMA GANDHI· ·IN 1903·

No. 16—Vol.-XLVIII. FRIDAY, 21ST APRIL, 1950

Indian Opinion

FRIDAY, 21ST APRIL, 1950

The African Problem

THE solution of the problem of the Africans is in the hands of the Africans themselves. The Africans in South Africa are in a similar position to the one in which four hundred million people of India were under the British rule. It is admitted that the economic structure of South Africa is dependent upon African labour. Similarly the economic structure of the British Empire was very largely dependent upon India. India was starved and bled to sustain the British Empire. The Africans are starved and bled in order to sustain white South Africa. India's progress could not be held back, however much they tried to do so. Continual suppression and oppression gave birth to discontent and frustration, which led the people to go mad and to succumb to the weaker nature of man—to resort to violence. That however did not help because superior forces of violence crushed their weaker forces and there was further suppression and oppression in a much harsher form—in the form of the historic Rowlatt Acts, which aimed at crushing individual liberty.

Then came on the scene one who taught India the use of another force which no physical or mechanical force, however great it may be, could crush. That was the force of love and non-violence taught by Mahatma Gandhi, and the world has seen, with great amazement, the result of that force. A similar thing is happening today in South Africa. The Africans are being suppressed and oppressed by harsh and inhuman laws. That has caused and is continuing to cause rapidly and in growing intensity discontent and frustration among them and they are beginning to lose themselves and are resorting to violent methods to seek relief. That, however, is not helping them just as it did not help the people of India. Much superior forces of arms are crushing their weaker forces and the suppression and oppression is being accelerated. Therefore the Africans too for their own freedom will have to learn to use the same weapon that the people of India successfully used for their salvation. They must learn to hate not the oppressor but oppression and must refuse to countenance oppression even at the risk of being tortured to death, without raising a finger against the oppressor. In order to do so they must develop moral and spiritual power. In fact the whole world needs to develop that power, which is far superior to the atom and the hydrogen bomb. We cannot develop that strength by leading a loose and an immoral life. Though we may be physically weak, morally and spiritually we must be so strong that the oppressor may break us but would not be able to bend us. In order to derive that strength they must abandon all intoxicating drinks, they must not indulge in women, they must not gamble, they must reduce the necessities of life to the barest minimum so that they can be self-supporting and need not have to be dependent upon anybody. Mankind has today become slave to the modern conveniences science has produced. Those conveniences have become a curse instead of a blessing. The Africans do not realise their potentialities. They have the power to stop, if they choose to, the whole machinery of the State but they cannot do so in their present state. If they desire to be happy they must first concentrate not on criticising the Government or the oppressors but on changing their way of life.

We are all today leading a life of complicity instead of simplicity, and the more we seek to increase our wants the more complicated our life becomes and brings in its trail more and more misery. Demonstrations, fiery speeches and all that outward show is decidedly not going to help us in the least. What is needed is real constructive work among ourselves of raising our moral and spiritual standard and making ourselves self-reliant. We Indians must help the Africans in this in every possible way. To challenge the Government and to go to prison is not all that we are expected to do. That will not bring the desired results unless we are ourselves pure in body, mind and soul. To talk of making common cause with the Africans and the other oppressed people sounds good, but we cannot do so unless we are ourselves qualified to fight our own cause. If we are then we should start fighting our own cause and thus set an example for others to follow. Our talk of making common cause with the Africans and the Coloureds to-day will rightly be interpreted as our wanting to exploit them to achieve our own end. If we feel for the African we must not drag him with us but help him in his own upliftment by practice rather than precept.

NOTES

Mr. A. Schauder On Racial Peace

Mr. A. Schauder of Port Elizabeth, who is a member of the National Housing Commission, addressing representatives of organisations interested in Native housing in Johannesburg last week said, Port Elizabeth had had to house 25,000 Africans in modern townships with full services and free medical attention. These people had formerly lived in Korsten, which he described as the worst slum in the world. People said that only a miracle could change the conditions of degradation that had accumulated for thirty years. That miracle had been accomplished in Port Elizabeth. The townships, one for Africans and one for Coloured people, had been built with Government money at three quarter per cent. interest and redemption over forty years. The entire township was policed by a hand-

Now confronted with an unexpected situation
They decided to drop the idea of the deputation
Chamberlain he could not meet
Nor beat a hasty retreat
So, George Godfrey now lead the deputation.

It bore no fruit, so they had to start anew.
The brickbats that he received were not few.
For helping in the war
When berated he felt sour
But that decision he never did rue.

All good action bears fruit, was his conviction.
So he banished all frustration
Got enrolled at Transvaal in the Supreme Court
Opening a law office, holding the fort
In Johannesburg filled with a moral intoxication.

Hurling himself in the service of the community
Found himself in the hub of frantic activity.
In 1904, the Indian location
In Johannesburg caught the infection
Of Pneumonic plague from a goldmine in the vicinity.

Hearing the news, he cycled to the location
Tending to the twenty-three victims, with determination.
Day and night
He did what was right
With his friends and Godfrey's kind cooperation.

But alas, only two of them could be saved
Gandhi and the rest, had all the risks braved.
With a new-found tenacity
He charged the municipality
With this calamity and a new path paved.

In 1904, he had tried his hand at journalism
Pouring his soul in the columns, with optimism.
Now, a friend Albert West
Took charge at his request
Infusing in this press at Durban new enthusiasm.

The *Indian Opinion* was at a loss, realised West
And informed Gandhi that he would try his best
Whether there was profit or not
The problem he would sort
Gandhi started for Durban, with *Unto This Last.*

From whose pages his eyes he could not unhook
And came under the magic spell of this book
Which a friend Polak had gifted
His spirits were uplifted
Mesmerized by the ideals of this gripping book.

Finding his deepest convictions reflected here
He decided to forge ahead without any fear.
Dignity of labour
And a life of labour
Were the principles that Ruskin held dear.

Phoenix Farm

Purchasing hundred acres of land for the office
Of the *Indian Opinion* he put them into practice.
Turning the wild land
With a committed band
Into a colony, he found nothing amiss.

Each worker was provided three acres of land
With earnest determination but no magic wand
A conducive environment
For moral upliftment
Came into being in 1904, on this plot of land.

On austere lines was the farm run
Enjoying moments in gay abandon
Far from peeved
By their labour they lived
With three pounds a month, alienating none.

Gandhi with Hermann Kallenbach and Sonia Schlesin

Every morning they manually ground the wheat
Laughter was not rare, when performing the feat.
On a hand-mill of seven pound
Was the wheat ground
Some shirked, others were relentlessly on their feet.

Of this farm, he was the patriarch benevolent
Far away from influences malevolent.
Cleaning, nursing, exercising
This was good training
For all the inmates active and indolent.

In February 1904 destiny played another hand
When the Zulus took a rebellious stand.
His sense of loyalty strong
To serve the Empire he did long
Not unaware of the Zulus' plight in their land.

In haste, he formed the Ambulance Corps
Reaching the scene with a party of twenty-four.
It was only a no-tax campaign
He realised with pain
The Zulus were flogged, senseless the gore!

Their arrival was hailed as a godsend.
Armed with first aid kits, they started to tend
To the Zulus injured
And had them cured
Happy were the Zulus that they had a friend.

They carried stretchers through difficult terrain
Man's cruelty, started a churning in his brain.
The hours of solitude
Changed his attitude
To serve his fellow men, he must strictly abstain.

He took the vow of celibacy, bringing exultation
Filling him with a fierce determination.
To observe Brahmacharya for life
He revealed to his wife
Now, deep he plunged into self-purification!

A New Challenge

Clouds gathered while this forecast hung in the air.
Their community was threatened, in a move unfair.
Full of resentment
His voice morally resonant
Pleaded negotiating with the opponent fair.

The Black and Brown could not be at par
With the White monopoly of power.
To get out of this fix
In August 1906
An ordinance was promulgated with repercussions far.

Everyone was to give thumb and finger impression
For getting compulsory registration
They were anguished
Afraid of being punished
If not registered, great would be their humiliation.

Gandhi with Indian community leaders in South Africa in 1905-08

On 11 September 1906 there was a mass meeting
With utter indignation people were seething.
To the Empire theatre people went
Which was taken on rent
Gandhi being the strategist behind this meeting.

Some were seated, others in the aisles stood
In this meeting the attendance was good.
Initially perplexed
About tackling the issue vexed
But soon he started frantically to brood.

The hall in Johannesburg was fully packed
Three thousand hearts with feelings racked.
Not to submit to the law unjust
Enraged they almost burst
Pained that the cards against them were stacked.

He would not haw he would not hedge
Come what may, he wouldn't violate his pledge.
With a new urgency sustained
Gandhi maintained
Exhilarated by the possibilities of this new pledge.

There'd be starvation, confiscation of property
Imprisonment, death, said he with intrepidity.
A violence free resistance
Was the essence
Of this movement for exploited Indian community.

Were the contours of a solution on course?
Gandhi was ambiguous about this discourse.
By a new intensity fired
This crusader untired
Behind the novel experiment was the moral force.

The circumstances against them were loaded
At Cape Town the Armadale Castle he boarded
To fight the passage of the Bill
All ready for the kill
In his mind many doubts exploded.

Although afflicted with a problem dental
Acutely alert were his faculties mental.
The crew members' punctuality
Exemplary humility
And the orderly discipline were not accidental.

Although they sailed forth with great enthusiasm
Haji Ojeer Ali was soon down with rheumatism
Subjected to baths cold and hot
Nursed and ordered about
Stoically, Ali endured the affectionate eccentricism.

In England six weeks he spent
Interacting with myriad hued people bent
Amidst the rampant strife
Dadabhai Naoroji was still full of life
This octogenarian was definitely not a force spent.

On his way back along the west coast of Africa
In the Portuguese island of Madeira
They received a telegram
Which acted as a balm
Joy spread, on receiving this cable in Madeira!

Cheerful tidings the cable did bring
The Bill had been vetoed by the King.
There were happy sighs
Dreams rippled in eyes
In the distance did a warning bell ring?

Their dreams shattered when they reached Cape Town
On his forehead appeared many an angry frown
His wrath he could not disguise
At this face saving device
He did not allow this to cow him down.

Without royal approval they reenacted the ordinance
Gandhi felt humiliated and absolutely tense
On 31st July 1907 it would go into force
Which was sheer injustice of course
Frantically, now they groped in a forest dense.

But he did not allow his spirits to dip down
Labelled the Black Act by people Black, Brown.
He fumed at this deception
But made a strong decision
To fight this blatant injustice in Cape Town.

Not to submit to the dog's collar, their determination
To never bow down before the humiliation
The authorities he approached
This topic he broached
Unfazed were the authorities by their imploration.

The British sense of justice he had always hailed
In October, with a delegate for London he sailed
Their hopes proved brittle
Alas, they achieved little
All of Gandhi's efforts had miserably failed.

To meet the challenge of this atrocity
Peaceful picketing started all over the city.
Indians refused to register
The wound continued to fester
And posters were displayed with impunity.

Indians, be free, they boldly proclaimed
Those who had felt insulted and maimed
Now opposed this outrage
And with a new courage
Refused to register, for which Gandhi was blamed.

By the authorities who resorted to every trick
To cow them down, they refused to panic.
The man brave but frail
Was taken to Johannesburg jail
For Smuts the situation was catastrophic!

Courageously, they started courting imprisonment
Jail became Edward Hotel, loving the environment.
They slept on the ground
A pleasure unusual found
In eating unpalatable food, harboring no resentment.

At dawn, Gandhi read the Gita, the Koran at noon
The two months in jail Gandhi considered a boon
Reading, writing and teaching
And a little bit of translating
He did with a passion, which ended soon.

In less than three weeks, came Albert Cartwright
An English journalist, sympathetic to India's plight.
He brought a draft from Smuts
Gandhi had no lack of guts
Venturing to do, what he thought was right.

If they registered voluntarily, it would be repealed
This understanding, Smuts and he sealed.
In human nature trust implicit
So he smelled no deceit
Before this compromise he willingly kneeled.

From registration, Smuts withdrew the compulsion
Which Gandhi felt had changed the situation.
He accepted voluntary registration
Some were filled with trepidation
Alam would kill the one who initiated registration!

Gandhi arranged to register despite the threat.
Outside his law office some Pathans he met
On 10th February 1908, who looked sinister
With companions he proceeded to register
He walked towards the bureau, all set.

Of selling himself to General Smuts accused.
His dilly dallying tactics had them confused.
Their ire could not be curbed
They were deeply perturbed
Vociferously they protested and even abused.

Some distance away from the office, waited a foe
On the top of his head, he received a heavy blow.
Who was this foe
Who had stooped so low?
Gandhi fell on the ground, kick followed blow.

Profusely bleeding, he was carried to a shop
Though in pain intense, he was no milksop.
The pain threatened to choke
On the scene came Joseph Doke
But Alam's arrest he could not stop.

Beseeched he that Mir Alam should be released
And he would not at all be pleased
If he were prosecuted.
In him forgiveness was deeprooted.
To this plea, Doke listened, not pleased.

Seething at this blow grossly unfair
Doke took him home for surgical care
In the lithe figure
With his clothes meagre
This Baptist Minister had found a friend rare.

By his earnest face he had been beguiled
But by his whims sometimes riled
For ten days, Gandhi was attended
And by the family lovingly mended
But often piqued by this doctor self-styled.

Although unwell, he was not made of clay
He wanted his fingerprints taken without delay.
Chamney, the registrar for Asiatics
Teary-eyed, was in a sad fix
As taking his fingerprints, was no child's play.

His teeth and ribs ached; cheek and lip stitched
With pain intense, this bag of bones twitched
The process hurt him physically
Moving the onlookers emotionally
Uncomplaining lay he, feeling spiritually enriched.

Dokes' daughter, Olive sang *Lead, Kindly Light.*
This never failed to fill Gandhi with delight.
Music filled his heart
With the will to restart
The Dokes' home was now a pilgrimage site.

People worried about their leader's health
Hastened to this man of meager wealth.
The millionaire and the pauper
And even the plain gawker
As someone played a game of stealth.

His recovery filling him with confidence.
He shifted to Polak's residence
Now, he went to Phoenix Farm
To see his family, in mind calm
Who were stunned after Alam's malevolence.

Not much later, Gandhi and even Cartwright gasped.
In anger, Gandhi's compatriots rasped.
At Gandhi's gullibility
And his credulity
As Smuts' wily nature he had not fully grasped.

Smuts' backtracking beyond comprehension
When he brazenly made clear his nasty intention
Of not repealing the Black Law
Gandhi realised the person's flaw
Without indulging in the backtracker's vilification.

The Indian community seethed in indignation
Vowing not to cower in spineless supplication.
On 16th August nineteen-hundred and eight
He called a meeting on this significant date
At Hamidra Mosque to oppose forced registration.

Onward surged they, their aims well-defined.
Towards a cauldron to defy the authorities' unkind.
In voices proud
Cheered the crowd
As registration certificates to the flame were consigned.

This was indeed an act of defiance untold
At which the authorities' blood ran cold.
They felt the heat
Of this fiery feat
A patriotic fervour made the Indians bold.

Up to him walked a man, six feet in height.
Was he bent on giving him a fright?
People watched in bated breath
In his gait, no stealth
He clasped Gandhi's hand in a grip tight.

In curiosity, forward the people surged.
He was Mir Alam Gir, now of rancour purged.
Apologetic of his impetuosity
Now filled with generosity
They shook hands, their interests converged.

Another law was passed by Transvaal legislature
Leading to Gandhi's intense discomfiture.
He wrote to the government
That the Satyagraha movement
Would now be aimed at this unjust measure.

As new immigrants from India it excluded
Over this injustice the community brooded.
Gandhi grew introspective.
In a tone accusative
Of raising new issues, by Smuts he was derided.

'Gandhi, when given an inch, asked for an ell.'
His accusation into the ears of irate Indians fell.
In indignation they grouped
Into the prisons they trooped
Prosperous people rushed to jail pell-mell!

Filled with patriotic fervour intense
Now started a process of hawking without licence.
This would surely not fail
To land them in jail
To the authorities, this made no sense.

In this second Satyagraha campaign
Authorities went all out to give them pain
Meting out harsh treatment
Which was spiritual upliftment
Smiling, they endured hardships of this terrain.

Why was he left alone, he wrote a letter.
Smuts had him arrested, Gandhi never felt better.
They tried to break his spirit
But made of grit
This man they failed to deter.

With criminals he spent the first night.
They were vicious, pathetic his plight.
But he kept his composure
The Gita giving pleasure
This man slight put up a brave fight.

In the Volksrust prison he was a prisoner ideal.
At times even preparing the meal.
To cooking he got hooked
The sugar-less porridge half cooked
Was lovingly eaten, though it held no appeal.

Seventy five compatriots answered his call.
Lodged in a small cell and not a huge hall.
The sanitary conditions crude
The prison authorities rude
He called himself the happiest man in Transvaal.

Surrounded by criminals of the worst sort
Never thinking that he was in a knot
Beaten and abused
Slapped and pushed
He endured all, in a vicious cycle caught.

Back bent, hands blistered he dug the ground
While an overseer ruthless, ominously frowned.
But none he feared
His companions he cheered
With his tenacity, the authorities he did astound.

His sentence ended on13th December 1908
Soon he was again outside the prison gate
To start a three-month sentence.
Five days later, in rain intense
For Pretoria he entrained, as dictated by Fate.

In the new local penitentiary to spend his term
His spirit unflagging and his resolve firm
This man of forty
With ideals lofty
Wrote letters, read during this three-month term.

He read Ruskin and Thoreau on Sundays
Stevenson and Carlyle, in a wondrous haze.
His energy did not drain
Many broke under the strain
Some laboured on, digging away with spades.

To get arrested in big numbers, their assertion
For the government, an expensive proposition.
To deal with this situation chaotic
Was adopted a device more drastic
Returning them, on compulsory repatriation.

As children, the labourers had come to this land
They knew South Africa, alien their motherland.
Seething in mortification
At this humiliation
Reluctant to go to India, for them a foreign land.

Such an attitude regrettable, Gandhi conceded.
Yet, he felt that his help was needed
By these people unfortunate
Who had been cheated by fate
With all his might their grievances he heeded.

Prison taught him altruism towards humanity
He took up cudgels on behalf of his community.
Taking the issue to the Supreme Court
Moral gumption keeping him afloat.
A steely strength now a trait of his personality.

By the court, illegal was declared this deportation
They exerted economic pressure and prosecution.
On the Indian community
Was heaped indignity upon indignity.
Causing them to lose faith in their agitation.

Swimming against the tide, a zeal he kindled
But alas, his loyal band alarmingly dwindled.
War weary felt his community
For him it was indeed a calamity
And he felt as though he was cruelly swindled.

No, they did not altogether give up the fight.
Some still forged ahead, with all their might.
Some grew restive
Under the measures punitive
Some abandoned the movement, ah sorry plight!

In the horizon, now a bigger danger loomed
Wondered the Indians, were they now doomed?
They grew inquisitive
And also apprehensive
Eyeing the horizon, while this hazard bloomed.

On 10 July nineteen hundred and nine
In England he arrived on a day fine
Meeting people eclectic
Who gaped at his activities hectic
Awe struck by this dynamo of a brilliant shine.

During his stay, he met people of every hue
Lord Morley, Lord Ampthill and Crewe
Worried about the Indians' plight
He worked day and night
But his visit proved fruitless, ah bitter brew.

Towards the end, he realised, to his ire
That about the pariahs of the Empire
The Whites were unconcerned
But the fire still burned
In him, though the circumstances were dire.

Tolstoy and Gandhi

In jail, in Tolstoy's books he found a soul-mate.
Greatly inspired by this man born in 1828.
War and Peace, Anna Karenina, Resurrection
Had brought him universal recognition
Between creed and conduct, synthesis he tried to create.

Tolstoy's doctrine was a source of attraction
Kingdom of God is within you, his assertion.
This inner kingdom Gandhi sought
Demons he valiantly fought
To Tolstoy he sent his first communication.

About his movement on 1st October 1909.
He replied immediately, his health not fine.
On 4th April nineteen hundred and ten
His second letter Gandhi did pen
To the man, whose health was on the decline.

Gandhi with his friends in South Africa in 1909

The Russian writer-philosopher Leo Tolstoy and the voracious reader, Gandhi, who was greatly influenced by Tolstoy (1907-8)

Hind Swaraj, accompanied his second letter
Which Tolstoy would critique, when he felt better.
From Yasnaya Polyana, Tolstoy wrote
Of passive resistance taking note
This was followed by Gandhi's third letter.

The Gandhi family and friends at the Tolstoy Farm in Johannesburg (1910-11). It was here that Gandhi's 'satyagraha', or non-violent resistence plan took shape

Tolstoy Farm

From England to South Africa Gandhi returned
At the end of 1909, with a new passion burned
To establish a rural commune
To city life, immune
And which material comforts spurned.

In the resisters he wanted austerity to ingrain
Phoenix Farm, was thirty miles by train.
The Transvaal struggle had to continue
But alas, the funds were few
Where to lodge their families, his worry main.

On 30th May 1910, the Satyagrahis were gifted
1,100 acres of land at Lawley, Gandhi's spirits lifted.
Hermann Kallenbach, a friendly German
Was the Good Samaritan
Who gifted this land, the Satyagrahis felt uplifted.

Twenty-one miles from Jo'burg, was Tolstoy Farm.
For Kallenbach and Gandhi family, a healing balm.
Amid fruit trees he became a baker
Caramel and marmalade maker
Rejuvenated by a spring and wells in ambience calm.

From all parts of India the residents hailed
And in their duties they never failed.
With Gandhi as guide
All the residents tried
Doing manual labour and their travails paled.

In his growth Tolstoy Farm was a milestone, pure
Where people poverty did cheerfully endure.
Here this man of sparse wealth
Wrote Guide to Health
Becoming a firm believer in nature cure!

In 1910, he wrote to Tolstoy about the farm.
Although depressed, the information was balm
It pleased the man ill
Who replied, still
Writing about uncorrupted love, in a tone calm.

The 82-year-old man suffering from ill health
At age 57, shunning his ancient title and wealth
Had embraced austerity
To serve humanity
Was, alas, now on the brink of death.

Not the one given to blind imitation
He revered this man who died at a railway station.
Hating violence and modern civilization
Bringing about a reconciliation
Between creed and deed his lifelong passion.

Even when wracked by unbearable pain
Tolstoy worried how the local peasantry would gain
To his heart so dear
Death was so near
He planned a station for them for collecting grain!

This landed proprietor turned wandering ascetic
Had held Gandhi under his spell hypnotic.
In anguish mental
His problem central
Was how to help mankind's condition so pathetic.

At the farm Gandhi was a satisfied peasant
In discipline monastic finding nothing unpleasant.
With his hands he worked
Ignoring the snakes that lurked
Digging the soil, plastering walls, finding life pleasant.

He ran a school based on the culture of the heart
In all this he played an active part.
Made the children valiant
Self-help the principle salient
The importance of manual work he also did impart.

The children felled trees, lifting loads with abandon
In making shoes, digging pits, finding nothing mundane.
There was discipline
And a happy din
Also picnics to Johannesburg which were fun!

In a monastery Kellenbach learnt sandal-making.
In a big way Gandhi took to cabinet-making.
Wood he hewed
Jackets he sewed
Which his wife wore without complaining.

To all, wooden pillows and blankets were provided.
In all this, the inmates were by Gandhi guided.
Without any revulsion
He supervised the sanitation
Prohibiting spitting, the inmates by the rules abided.

Once this nonviolent man resorted to violence
For the aberration of others, he did penance.
He struck an unruly boy
But derived no joy
Disarming everyone by his child-like innocence.

In Kallenbach, he found a partner in experimentation
Who now cheerfully shared every deprivation
All meals light
And a fruitarian diet
Both followed, without the slightest irritation.

The Satyagrahis were being subjected to humiliation.
In India, this news was causing intense devastation.
The cause by Gokhale espoused
A patriotic fervour aroused
Round the corner was George V's coronation.

In early 1911 the wily South African government
Took to the path of appeasement
Of these Indians irate
The latter fell for this bait
Which in February 1911 resulted in an announcement.

The racial bar would be removed, they said
In this tale, there was a twist unread.
An education test severe,
Prohibited Indians here
With trickery they were misled.

In October 1912 Gokhale came as guest.
To be always at his side, Gandhi tried his best.
During his one month stay
Gandhi as secretary and valet
Ironed and creased the scarf of this state guest.

Given a royal welcome by the Indian community
Gokhale had no doubts about the government's veracity
The meeting was a farce
And honesty sparse
The government pledge hid its mendacity.

After the meeting Gokhale naively believed
That that Black Act would surely be repealed
And also the tax of three pound
They had broken new ground
As he set sail for India he felt relieved.

To return to India in a year Gandhi he asked
While in this triumph premature, he basked.
Gandhi the pledge doubted
Knowing it would be flouted
Soon enough their intentions were unmasked.

No sooner Gokhale left, Smuts announced his inability
To abolish the tax, mocking Indian credulity!
Guts they lacked
Brazenly back-tracked
In Gandhi and his band, of grit there was no scarcity.

In the Bai Mariam case, the judiciary invalidated
Marriages according to Christian rites not celebrated.
This was another bombshell
On 14 March 1913 which fell
In rage they seethed, feeling utterly degraded.

The women felt their honor was at stake
From their stupor shaken, now wide awake.
This affront outrageous
Made them furious
Into the fray they jumped, for honor's sake!

They resolved through this unusual movement
To alter the spirit of the government
Gokhale was bemused
And somewhat confused
How 66 Satyagrahis could alter the government!

He began his struggle in September, nineteen thirteen.
And sent a party of volunteers sixteen
From Phoenix farm in Natal
Without permit they entered Transvaal
And were arrested on September 23rd, nineteen thirteen.

Women now crossed in the reverse direction.
Reaching New Castle from Tolstoy Farm, sans permission.
Miners put down their tools
The authorities, were no fools
Relentlessly they pursued their course of repression.

For three months the women were put in jail
In curbing their spirit, the government did fail.
Indignation flared
More people dared
Shrugging away the hardships which it did entail.

The government turned off water and light
For the miners this was hardship slight.
The strike spread
Cautious his tread
From Phoenix Farm to boost the fight.

Under the mine owners' threats no one flinched
By Gandhi's moral leadership, they felt enriched
Guided by this slight figure
With their belongings meager
Outside the Lazarus' house their camps they pitched.

There were 5,000 strikers outside the house
To Whites' grievances was added one more grouse.
They were vexed
Gandhi was perplexed
What to do with the rabble outside the house!

He urged the coal miners to return to the mines
Yet they refused to think on those lines.
Faith in him immense
It made no sense
Firmly resolved not to go back to the mines!

On his shoulders now an immense responsibility
He hit upon a strategy with great alacrity.
To deposit them safely in jail
This, he thought wouldn't fail
13th October 1913 was set by this man of integrity.

On this day, the homeless people Brown
Would march from New Castle to Charlestown.
Into the Transvaal to walk
To render a knock
And court arrest, their brows free of frown.

Each soldier with a pound and a half of bread
An ounce of sugar, determination in his tread.
Some with babies in their arms
These soldiers with no arms
Walked on, spines straight, purged of dread.

His colleagues Polak, Kallenbach, Ms Schlesin
Also formed part of this rabble and din.
Full of moral might
On a starvation diet
Convinced, protesting against injustice was no sin!

Charlestown they reached in days two
The pilgrims appeared a picturesque crew.
On legs spindly they walked
But these thin legs rocked
The government, which wondered, what to do.

On 6th November 1913 they marched across the border
They were tired, but still did not dodder
With incredible fortitude
The poor but brave multitude
Marched on but stopped short of the border.

For Gandhi, it was now the moment
To write to the unrepentant government
With withering contempt
His mail was dealt
And no response came from a government arrogant.

Now, he rang up Smuts as a last resort
His secretary, appeared to be of a temper hot
Retorted, 'do as you please'.
Gandhi's brows did crease
Were their efforts coming to naught?

It was not the marchers' intention
To settle in Transvaal, this he wanted to mention
They would end the movement
If there was an improvement
The tax abolished, removing their apprehension.

Against their breach of faith, it was a protest
This, he conveyed to the government to his best
But it was full of rage
At the blatant outrage
Of the marchers on the path of a protest!

Trouble was expected at Volksrust, a village
Where, the Europeans had threatened carnage.
To shoot them like rabbits had vowed
But the pilgrims uncowered
Marched on, and crossed this border village.

This meeting, Kallenbach had also attended
And, the Indians he had stoutly defended
To fire this had acted as fuel
He was challenged to a duel.
But this pacifist forged ahead, unoffended.

They vowed to walk on unaffected by gunfire
Proposing to melt hearts and their ire
Hence none fought
No one was shot
They strove on, though circumstances were dire!

Untired in spirit, at Palmford they made the first stop.
Cheered constantly by their leader, who, was no milksop
Beyond Volksrust Palmfort was mile eight
On the ground they stretched out as it was late.
Gandhi heard some footsteps. Was it a cop?

His ears pricked, was someone snickering?
In the distance there was a light flickering
Then he saw a man
Was he a policeman?
He came forward, light still flickering.

In a polite tone, said he, 'I want to arrest you'.
Gandhi woke a faithful lieutenant, PK Naidoo.
The march should continue
He told Naidoo
Towards Tolstoy Farm they marched with vigour new.

While his faithful lieutenant, held the fort
He was taken to Volksrust and tried in court.
The prosecutor wanted jail
But he was released on bail
Furnished by Kallenbach, on whom he did dote.

In a car, which Kallenbach had kept ready
He was driven to his marchers to get steady.
With hatred toward none
With no missile or gun
They strove on still further, their fervour heady!

Of this pacific multitude, Gandhi was the head
With exemplary moral courage, they were lead.
Fifty-seven children, 127 women
And 2,037 committed men
Had vowed to march, to stop only when dead!

The next day the caravan halted at Standerton
The pilgrims marched on, under the sun.
While distributing bread and marmalade
He was accosted by a magistrate
Once again was imprisoned the Brave One.

'Magistrates take the trouble to arrest me', he quipped
He beamed at the promotion, magistrate was tightlipped.
Again he was freed on bail
Five co-workers were sent to jail
Rued the authorities, the evil had not been nipped.

On 9th November, at the head of a column
Gandhi and Polak walked, not feeling glum
Up to them came a cart
Time again to part?
There was an officer in the cart, why had he come?

To Polak, Gandhi handed command when told of arrest.
He informed the marchers, who were doing their best.
Remain peaceful, his army he told
'Make no speeches', the officer shouted in a voice cold.
In four days, this was Gandhi's third arrest!

Kallenbach he found in the jail confined
Gandhi was brought to trial which he didn't mind.
Although guilty he pleaded
His plea went unheeded
He was requested, against himself, a witness to find!

Kallenbach, Polak and Gandhi mutually testified
Leaving the high ups absolutely mystified.
It was a strange phase
The authorities were in a daze
Judge Jooste, in utter frustration, sighed.

Giving them three months hard labour in prison
From where he wrote letters, on many an occasion.
The peace warriors increased
The Whites' confidence decreased
To Bloemfontein he was shifted from Volksrust prison!

Lodged in a cell ten feet long, seven feet wide
Permission to walk in this cell he was denied.
He did not grumble
And did not crumble
Nor did the authorities he deride.

Denied a bench in the cell darkness replete.
He was a picture of stoic composure neat.
When summoned in a court case
With not a grimace on his face
He walked, undeterred by the manacled feet!

The miners were carried back to the mines by train
And forced to resume work under great strain.
They received whips and sticks
And also vicious kicks
When they refused to work suffering intense pain.

At this policy, India fumed in humiliation
Filling Viceroy Hardinge with exasperation.
A commission of inquiry he demanded
The South African government he derided
And was outspoken in his public condemnation!

On the wrong foot, Smuts had been caught
With great danger the situation was fraught
In a gesture dramatic
In rebellion sympathetic
More indentured labourers struck work in temper hot!

The meagre statistics that had Gokhale bemused
Had now gigantic proportions assumed.
The trickle was now a deluge
Gandhi had a peace force huge
Of indentured labourers, the Whites were unamused!

To inquire into grievances, a Commission was appointed.
Their disapproval at its White membership they reiterated.
This policy of carrot and stick
Was meant only to hoodwink
For the next step, breath bated, everyone waited.

Soon, Gandhi, Polak and Kallenbach were released
By this release, the trio was displeased
The Whites thought this would testify
And to their intentions give the lie
With this move wily, they were highly pleased.

Gandhi did not doubt Chairman Solomon's integrity
But Esselen, against the Indians had an animosity
The Commission's third member
Gandhi did painfully remember
Had led an anti-Indian mob with brazen audacity.

Gandhi suggested Commission reconstitution
Gokhale sent Pearson, Andrews for mediation.
The situation with anxiety fraught
Gandhi was bent on boycott
An enraged Hardinge pleaded for moderation.

To the threat of a march over Smuts' head
Was added another crisis filling him with dread.
Workers of South African Railways, all White
Went on a strike. Ah, sorry plight!
Set to carry out the boycott, Gandhi cancelled it, instead!

It wasn't the tactics of Satyagraha philosophy
To take advantage of someone's difficulty
To conquer the heart
This formed a part
Of Gandhi's sublime and sincere philosophy.

Refusing to turn Smuts' calamity into opportunity
He called off the march, in absolute humility.
Though his camp didn't endorse
For an inquiry he did not force
Thus reconciliation followed mutual hostility.

His opponents, resentful and stiff-upper-lipped
Buckled under this strategy sublime and flipped.
Though a little late
Smuts agreed to negotiate
Was the issue of racial inequality finally nipped?

Anxious about hostility to South African persecution
On a steamer came Sir Benjamin Robertson
Extraordinary envoy
Of Hardinge, the Viceroy
Whose image had risen after Smuts' condemnation.

The negotiators were in the grip of a verbal war
Honing, weighing phrases, removing any flaw.
The excluded
Was finally included
And in July 1914 the Bill became South African law.

The Transvaal agitation against racial discrimination in 1913

Hindu, Muslim, Parsi marriages it validated
The three pound tax would be abolished, it stated.
Both sides were pleased
Mutual rancour decreased
Better sense on the Whites' prevailed, though belated.

Of civil resistance this triumph was a vindication.
Despotisms would be abolished, the indication.
Smuts was checkmated
Gandhi was feted
Not to rest on his laurels, his determination.

The law hailed as Magna Carta, in this land.
He yearned to go back to his motherland.
Though still under the magic
Of the British Empire historic
In passive resistance he had a weapon grand!

Gandhi and associates with community members after they were released from South African jails

Farewell, God-forsaken Land

On 18th July 1914 the couple, aged five plus forty
Winning the fight with the government haughty
For England Gandhi sailed
Having the government nailed
Which had so brazenly supported racial inequality.

To him South Africa had become a sacred land
For which his love was next only to his motherland
With a heavy heart
From his friends he did part
By Kallenbach accompanied they sailed for England.

Kallenbach for binoculars had an infatuation
Two costly pairs he had in his possession
Where was the necessity
If the goal was simplicity
For such costly items to have an obsession?

Thus reasoned Gandhi, the simple soul
'Throw them away, ' said he, austerity his goal.
Fling the things away
Kallenbach did say
Gandhi threw the field glasses out the porthole!

Never inclined to broaden any rift
On his departure, to Smuts he gave as gift
A pair of sandals made in jail
In its aim, it didn't fail.
In Pretoria, Smuts lovingly wore this gift of thrift.

On 2nd October 1939, when Gandhi turned seventy
He returned the gift to him in all amiability.
Gandhi he had derided
Later he confided
That such men redeem human beings from futility.

He had worn them for many summers since then
Was unworthy to stand in the shoes of so great a man.
This remark magnanimous
Came from a man who once was mendacious
But was by now a world famous statesman.

Into the English Channel; now entered the ship
A sudden crisis the world did grip
On 4th August the First World War broke out
Now Gandhi was in no doubt
To throw his lot with the British Empire in this hardship.

Through mines, the ship was towed, in this crisis
The channel they crossed two days after this.
On 6th August nineteen fourteen
To meet Gokhale, Gandhi, who was very keen,
Was informed, he had been stranded in Paris!

Not to throw his lot with Britain at war, friends did plead
But to this argument, Gandhi paid no heed.
It made no sense
To sit on the fence
He believed that a friend in need is a friend indeed.

Yes, Gandhi still treated Britain as a friend
This on many an occasion, he had boldly said.
It was neither just nor righteous
Said this man credulous
To take advantage of a country which he regarded as friend.

To take advantage even of an enemy in distress
This line of thinking did not impress
The man veracious
Who could never be malicious
Even to an enemy who had put him in a mess!

Gandhi had succeeded in quelling the fear
Under first aid training was put every volunteer
To be followed by military drill
They had no time to kill
Even diligently stitching clothes to wear!

Due to the severe cold to go home he was advised.
Which he accepted, his reluctance he disguised
Clinging to fruits and nuts
Shrugging away all 'buts'
Gokhale had already left for home, not ill advised.

Kallenbach wanted to go to India by the same boat
Being a German, his passport was in doubt
Which the government denied
His grief he couldn't hide
That he couldn't go to India in the same boat!

With 'Medes' plaster Gandhi's ribs were bandaged
With this, he felt uncomfortable and caged
For days two he bore
The pain feeling sore
Now, he undid the plaster, and somehow a bath managed!

The Englishman did not consider Indians at par
On his mind this observation painfully did jar.
Surviving on fruit and nuts
Despite the pain, he showed guts
And now sang his heart, as Bombay was not far!

Gandhi in India
January 1915

On 9th January 1915, they reached Bombay
Welcomed warmly at the Apollo Bandur that day
In a mood introspective
He was also apprehensive
Happy was Pherozeshah, the uncrowned king of Bombay.

But, alas to him India was a strange country
Although, he had returned as a celebrity
Sadly out of his element
He felt in the alien environment
Profoundly he missed his South African community!

It was in April 1893 that a young barrister perplexed
And with the rampant corruption morally vexed
Finding himself at an end loose
Had started to muse
Worried, what was in store for him next.

Gandhi back in Bombay in 1915

This dilemma, the 24-year-old couldn't bear
A Muslim firm, offered to send him there
His heart began to sing
When this lawsuit big
Came his way, he could not spurn this offer so rare.

He couldn't forego this tempting opportunity
Of earning wealth, and seeing a new country
He would make it big
A fortune he would bring
On his young shoulders, a heavy responsibility.

To help in the expenses of the household
The young diffident youth, took this step bold
Faced with an unpleasant situation
To pursue his ambition
In this land unknown, would he strike gold?

Yes, this man, in South Africa did strike gold
Turning the diffident, cowardly youth into a man bold
With all his moral might
He stood for the right
Winning more and more people into his loving fold.

He was returning to India as a great celebrity
As a man who had shown courage and integrity
He was widely feted
Smuts he had defeated
By the potent weapons of nonviolence and veracity.

Gandhi with family members in Ahmedabad in 1915

In England, war led to his unexpected detention
As he landed in Bombay, heady with moral intoxication
In his face stared a question
What about his obligation
To the Phoenix party already at its destination?

Would his country accept him, was his apprehension
With many a doubt his head reeled in tension
He was all tangled
His notions new-fangled
Whirled in his mind, seeking a new dimension!

With his dhoti, turban and Kathiawadi cloak
He was the cynosure of common and uncommon folk
With misgivings replete
A rustic complete
Felt the returning Indian, at times about to choke.

Everywhere this man of destiny was warmly feted
As the great Gandhi he was universally greeted
To them he was a hero.
But he felt like a zero
When like a long lost son of his country he was treated.

As the heroine of South Africa they did hail
Gandhi's better half in plain saree, who looked frail
Some found Gandhi eccentric
And some quixotic
But in arousing all-round curiosity he did not fail.

Twenty-eight years, he viewed India with alien eyes
From far, things looked bright, and nice
His roots he had lost
Dear was the cost
Unheard had gone the violent rumbling and the sighs!

Willingdon offered him an audience
Till then, faith in the British was his sustenance
There was no altercation
But mutual satisfaction
He had no reason to question the British beneficence.

With India he was woefully out of touch
Of its socio-political condition he didn't know much
Following Gokhale's suggestion
Of a year's probation
With his country's condition, he tried to get in touch.

On a sure guide, he could now depend
Gokhale would help this weakness to amend
No time to waste
He soon made haste
To Poona to meet his guide and friend.

In 1905, Gokhale founded The Servants of India Society
Which regarded itself above moral laxity
Gokhale was keen
And did sincerely mean
To make Gandhi a member of this society.

But not all members shared Gokhale's view
He was uncompromising, they knew
Although, by Gokhale favoured
By many, the idea was ill-savoured
Being apprehensive about this person new.

Gandhi was also well-versed with his own nature
So, to ease everyone's intense discomfiture
In a decision prudent
At the last moment
He willingly withdrew his candidature.

Gandhi was now more than forty-five years of age
He said he yearned to have his own hermitage
On the lines of Phoenix Farm
So it came as a balm
When Gokhale offered funds at this stage.

Youngsters from Phoenix Farm were at Shantiniketan
Where wanted to hasten this Indian son
It was a vibrant community
Where in great congeniality
Hundred and twenty five pupils lived under the sun.

At his departure, a party was hosted in his farewell
Gokhale was on bed, feeling quite unwell
Gandhi was filled with gloom
As Gokhale was ill in his room
But, suddenly everything was pell-mell.

Everyone sprang up, immediately on the guard
Who was it staggering across the courtyard?
With strength meager
A ghostly figure
Took a few steps and collapsed in the courtyard!

Gokhale wanted to give him a tribute affectionate
For his frail body, this was an effort great
Everyone was harried
To his bed he was carried
The party must go on, said his mentor and mate.

Gandhi in Shantiniketan with Rabindranath Tagore

Shantiniketan

Shantiniketan was his next destination
Which he visited with a new determination
Overwhelmed with affection
At a simple reception
He was filled with great exhilaration.

Dwijendra Nath welcomed him to the community
The younger brother away from this fraternity.
At the peaceful Shantiniketan
He met Andrews and Pearson
His friends, who taught in pristine tranquility.

In the dusty plains of Bolpur, it had been set
Soon this experimental school become a prized asset
Where the students' creativity
In great felicity
Flowered, nourishing the minutest facet.

Here he spent an eventful week
To many questions answers he did seek
Under his persuasion
And affectionate supervision
They cooked, enjoying his remarks tongue-in-cheek.

Mulling over changes, like a student wise
He followed his mentor Gokhale's advice
Mouth shut, he watched Argus eyed
Restless about his guide
His anxiety over his illness he could ill disguise.

Like a thunderbolt, came a telegram
Which wreaked havoc with the ambience calm
Gandhi felt utterly lost
In an ocean storm tossed
His mentor had died, colossal the harm.

In him Gandhi had found a pilot, for sure
In his keeping, he confessed, he had felt secure.
The same day
In a mood gray
Kasturba and he headed for Poona, feeling insecure.

After the memorial service, to Shantiniketan he returned
With a reformative zeal, he now burned
In the atmosphere calm
Tagore and Gandhi moved arm-in-arm
In discussing India's future, many things they learned.

Two days later, to Calcutta the band proceeded
Gandhi was free to pursue the reforms, much needed.
Into a monastic community
He wanted to turn Tagore's fraternity
Much to Andrew's disapproval, which he hardly heeded.

The great soul in beggar's garb
Remained unruffled by any barb
A meeting he called
Shantiniketan he overhauled
Andrews was irate with his friend in beggar's garb!

Bitterly arguing, but to his whim he did bow
For, his eccentric friend, he really did love
The system of sanitation
Needed renovation
To follow his instructions he asked them to take a vow.

They ran the kitchen, and handled the garbage
Some smilingly, some boiling with rage
The Brahmin cooks were sacked
As cleanliness they lacked
They marveled at his fads, hiding their outrage!

At his eccentricities, Tagore merrily chuckled
Under Andrews' barbs, Gandhi never buckled
This new craze
Lasted forty days
When Gandhi left Shantiniketan, it quietly buckled.

Gandhis at the Sabarmati Ashram, 1917

Gandhi and the New Hermitage

By going barefoot for a year, Gokhale he mourned
For the rampant corruption, he atoned
Across the length and breadth he traveled
Appalled at his country bedeviled
At the social evils, he inwardly moaned.

He visited Burma, and Hardwar to see the Kumbh fair
The fraudulent priests he found grossly unfair
The prevailing untouchability
The Hindus' superiority
And the spiritual degeneration, he couldn't bear.

His heart burdened by the Hardwar pilgrimage
Now he craved for some peaceful anchorage
There were many choices
And myriad voices
He settled for Ahmedabad to found his hermitage.

His frantic search came to a fruitful end
Of many reasons, his final choice, a happy blend
At Kochrab near Paldi
Settled Mohandas Gandhi
In Jivan Lal Desai's bungalow, his barrister friend.

Of invitations for founding the ashram, there was no dearth
But Gandhi thoughtfully chose the place of his birth.
Ahmedabad was a textile centre
Many a financial mentor
Offered to finance his ashram in the place of his birth.

What should they name this ashram based on frugality
Which had a mere population of five and twenty?
After serious deliberation
They reached a final selection
Satyagraha Ashram they would call this new community.

The building, for community life was ill-designed
The outbreak of plague was also a blow unkind
The inmates' number soared
Now Gandhi could not afford
To live in this building, offered by the barrister kind.

Now, after two years, they shifted to a permanent site
On the Sabarmati bank where he led many a fight
This Spartan accommodation
Witnessed Gandhi's evolution
From a lawyer to a Mahatma of majestic might!

The ashram covered an area of acres hundred and fifty
Where the inmates were expected to be austere and thrifty.
In this site new
Were built cottages few
Soon this ashram became a beehive of activity.

Here millions came under his hypnotic spell
To this champion spinner, people ran pell-mell
Staff in hand this scrawny figure
With clothes meager
Would someday trigger the Empire's death knell.

The ashram had a school, library and dining room
Many an inmate could be seen wielding a broom
For Gandhi, cleanliness
Was next to godliness
And a place central, occupied the loom!

Plans he had many, to Magan Gandhi fell their execution
To South African settlements, immense his contribution
With his practical ability
And staunch loyalty
He turned the ashram into a thriving organisation.

In the pulse of the ashram, Hridyakunj Gandhi stayed
For sixteen years here, many a plan was laid
Vows of truth, nonviolence, charity
Non-stealing, fearlessness, anti-untouchability
Were administered, he saw to it that none strayed.

Graduates of foreign universities young and old
Sanskrit scholars, girls and boys, meek and bold
Also cynics thinly-disguised
This group comprised
Two hundred and thirty inmates came into its fold.

In the darkness, the ashram was a bright spark
Where Gandhi ruled as a benevolent patriarch
This community proud
Far from the madding crowd
With its simple living and high thinking created a mark.

In this calm, was heard a storm rumbling
Were the Mahatma's ideals, all-a-crumbling?
Some inmates were unhappy
That an untouchable family
Into the ashram was admitted, there was grumbling!

The wealthy merchants seethed at this outrage
They cut off the funds boiling with rage
Gandhi was utterly distraught
Caught in a bewildering knot
His overburdened heart took umbrage.

As a solution to this unprecedented matter
He decided to shift to the untouchables' quarter
In the slums of Ahmedabad
And labour hard
To sustain themselves in the untouchables' quarter!

From Ahmedabad now came Ambalal Sarabhai
When all doors were closed, and no help was nigh
Rupees 13,000 he gave as donation
Gandhi was filled with elation
The crisis over, he heaved a relieved sigh!

But now, he faced a crisis more difficult
To his ideals indeed a gross insult
The untouchables' arrival
Had led to a revival
Of Ba's untouchability bias, creating a tumult.

Give up untouchability or quit, Ba he told
In a voice which was brutally cold
This was no threat hollow
Tears she did swallow
Accepting the family into the ashram's fold.

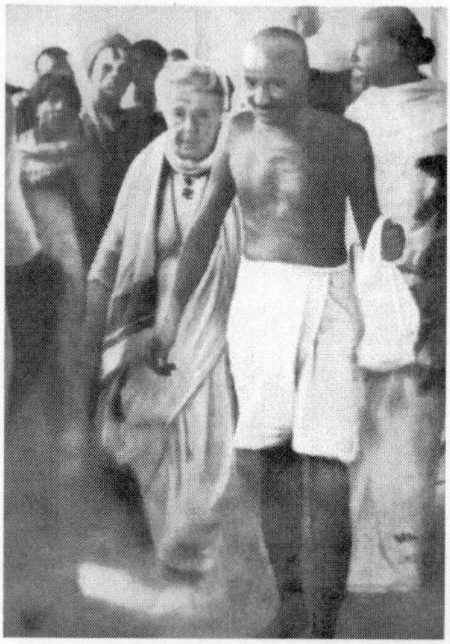

Gandhi with the theosophist Anne Besant (top); Gandhi with Swami Shraddhanand (bottom)

Annie Besant and Gandhi

In this period, Annie Besant had dominated the stage
A speaker eloquent she had formidable courage
Gifted with an incisive mind
In 1916, this lady kind
Founded the Home Rule League, seventy years her age.

She had not enlisted his support for her movement
As she thought it would embarrass the government
'The moment of England's difficulty
Is the moment of India's opportunity,'
Such statements from Besant filled him with resentment.

The Hindu college in Banaras, she had founded
In 1892, soon it became well-entrenched and grounded.
A quarter century later
This revolutionary educator
Saw the granting of University status to the college founded.

For her in February 1916, came a moment of joy
When Banaras University was opened by the Viceroy
Besant resplendent in white
Was an awe-inspiring sight
On the dais, among dignitaries beaming with joy.

In this function, in his half-naked glory, Gandhi strode
Amidst the bedecked noblemen, of a weird mould.
Princes and officials wealthy
Dignitaries robust and healthy
From the dais, gave the frail figure, looks cold.

When bedecked Maharajas spoke of India's poverty
Gandhi delivered some home truths with impunity.
Princes bejeweled
Their breaths held
As Gandhi hurled indignity upon verbal indignity!

To strip themselves of jewelry, they were admonished
Some were stunned, and some merely astonished.
The atmosphere electric
Soon became chaotic
When he plunged forth, with his speech unvarnished!

The cynics the credentials of the man doubted
Their mouths fell, as courtesy, he said, he had flouted.
The students were enthused
Others were confused
'Here, hear', the youth in the audience shouted!

'We may foam, we may fret…', he vented steam
Tall amidst the dwarfs, masquerading as society's cream
Some princes left the dais
Huffing at his anti-princes bias
To a nightmare was reduced their roseate dream!

'Please stop it', an embarrassed Besant pleaded
He had already delivered the dose much needed
Some audibly moaned
The meeting was adjourned
In helplessness, others their hands kneaded.

In his first public address he had exploded
His moral armoury with verbal punches, well-loaded
No more on a year's probation
Worried about India's salvation
With vigour, the scantily-clad figure had thus exploded.

Gandhi leading his initial satyagrahas in India, 1918, Champaran (Bihar)

Satyagraha 1918

Keen-eyed Gandhi watched India's political situation
Trying to clean his mind of the cobwebs of confusion
Armed with an instrument effective
It was now his objective
To right the wrongs with his powerful ammunition.

In Champaran, Bihar there was agrarian discontent
For a century, peasants had seethed in resentment
With a determination tenacious
The man labourious
Now forayed into this significant assignment.

Relations between planters and peasants were hostile
The Indian cultivators finding European owners vile
Raj Kumar Shukla, a peasant
To him disclosed the fact unpleasant
Following itinerant Gandhi for more than a mile.

Indigo factories were set up in the 19th century
Soon becoming peasants' source of impotent fury
In indigo cultivation
There was exploitation
The Tinkathia System the reason of this righteous fury.

Under the system there was an unjust agreement
European planters with the peasants had an arrangement
Under which they reeled.
Three twentieths of the best yield
Was cheaply bought by owners under this agreement.

In the beginning of 20th century, Indigo cultivation fell
German industry, blowing natural indigo's death knell.
Synthetic indigo
Drove natural indigo
From the market, everything was pell-mell!

The planters now decided to take quick action
Releasing the tenants from the earlier obligation
Showing cunning and duplicity
They made a virtue of necessity
But this release was no cause for celebration.

Now the planters started levying illegal extraction
For not growing indigo they demanded compensation.
On the wrong foot caught
The peasants were distraught
They started beating their heads in frustration!

The peasants' spirits were on the descent
As the rents shot up by almost sixty per cent
Into this scene chaotic
Walked a maverick
Who realised the folly of being complacent!

To the headquarters of Champaran district, Motihari
With a single-minded concentration went Gandhi
At the things learned
With a fire he burned
To Motihari went a determined Gandhi!

Leave the district by the next train, he was told
Unheeded went the order by the man bold
With the situation tainted
He got thoroughly acquainted
Trying to rectify the condition under which they groaned.

For this, he was tried on 18 April, nineteen-seventeen
But this warrior had a conscience clean
He had disregarded the order
Not to create disorder
But only to keep his conscience clean!

He was arrested by Commissioner of Tirhut Division
But, with his superior he had no consultation
The government of Bihar was pained
As it later explained
That this was a serious mistake in line of action!

They stopped proceedings against this man of integrity
He was given every reasonable facility
The peasants earlier outraged
Now, were fully assuaged
To continue his investigation, Gandhi now at liberty!

Armed with rich experience, the apostle of nonviolence
Boosted them by his mere presence
Now their liberator
This impartial investigator
Moved forward with a lethal common sense.

Inquiries he conducted with vigour indefatigable
Studying local problems, collecting facts indisputable
In his possession
A large mass of information
Now for the peasants he made a case irresistible!

The planters were shocked, the peasant filled with elation
Just round the corner, was a major transition.
The government was perturbed
And positively disturbed
What if the peasants started a Satyagraha agitation!

The government appointed the Champaran committee
In which a seat was also offered to Mohandas Gandhi.
Who was knowledgably persuasive
And sensitively perceptive
The abolition of Tinkathia was recommended by the committee!

With regard to illegal exaction
A twenty-five per cent refund was its recommendation
This triumph strategic
Made the peasants euphoric
A thing of the past was now their inhuman oppression!

Realising that the root of trouble was ignorance
A literacy mission he started with great patience
In full swing in Champaran
There were lessons in sanitation
Teachers swept the roads setting examples in civic sense!

Steeped in dirt and extreme poverty
Purdah was in vogue, so was untouchability
With untiring zeal imbued
His goal he pursued
Some mystified by this man, they found an oddity.

In his cap the Champaran feather
He was not at the end of his tether
He could not rest
There was another test
So, head on, he forayed into the turbulent weather.

Gandhi was elected President of the Indian National Congress in 1919 and 1920, as well as the All India Home Rule League. Seen here are women training for the League.

Textile Workers' Strike

The cauldron of textile industry was on bubble
The workers' dreams were about to be reduced to rubble
Discontent simmered
But a hope glimmered
For Gandhi would now address this trouble.

Since August 1917, a plague bonus they had received
But now, they were absolutely peeved
They wrung their hands in despair
Finding it utterly unfair
That by the employers they were being deceived!

Discontinue the bonus, the employers decided
This decision the workers derided
The times were troubled
The cost of living had doubled
On a drastic remedy they now decided.

'Don't go back to work', Gandhi emphasised
For this, the nonviolent crusader was criticised
The mill-owners gritted their teeth
At the workers' dubious feat
And poured scorn on the workers all-sized.

Every day on the Sabarmati bank under a babool
The workers met in the ambience cool
In environment neat
With discipline complete
The unarmed warrior tried to disarm, without ridicule.

In joyous approval, the birds their wings flapped
The workers listened in attention rapt
Mutual regard, he emphasized
The employers' ire ill-disguised
Burst forth in news-sheets, labeling the interference inapt.

With no rancour they performed activities constructive
With a zest new, learning trades alternative
Without nursing grouses
They repaired houses
And swept roads, shunning ill-will and invective.

On witnessing the rampant sickness and starvation
Gandhi was filled with exasperation
Had he been naïve
Could one survive
Without wages and work, his apprehension.

Though on the brink of disaster they teetered
Gandhi was not the one to be deterred
He forged ahead
The mill-owners saw red
Unfazed, the workers marched on the streets filth littered.

On 15 March 1918, under the babool the crowd was small
The Satyagrahi was filled with gall
Would the strike collapse
Under some inadvertent lapse?
Then light dawned- in this light, he saw all.

'I will not touch any food', the man declared
The workers were dumbstruck; for him they cared
With hands folded they pleaded
Their pleas went unheeded
The strike must go on, thus his views he aired.

Sincerely, he swore by Ruskin's *Unto This Last.*
Guilt ridden were the workers by his intention to fast
Without any half-truths or lies
The workers he wanted to mobilise
For the mill-owners, the sky was overcast.

Against the workers the owners threatened action
They were rightly filled with wrathful exasperation
A union of elephants
Against a union of ants
Was the fearless Satyagrahi's instant reaction.

Satyagraha was the only weapon in his armoury
To organise a nonviolent strike he was in a hurry
Rendering the healing touch
He did much
Paving the road for a final victory.

He took up cudgels on the workers' behalf
For this warrior, this was no job tough
In platitudes he did not dabble
Nor did he rouse the rabble
The employers panicked, but he had the last laugh!

After three days fast, Gandhi accepted a compromise
Mutual expectations were now on the rise
The employers yielded to arbitration
Filling the workers with elation
Thirty five per cent was won in a pleasant surprise!

Gandhi in Kheda
March 1918

The crusader could not rest on his laurels
Well shielded by an armoury of morals
This man of unusual grit
Now headed for Kheda district
His mission to rip rancour and stop quarrels.

Here the peasantry was hit by a draught severe
Making them shed many a silent tear
The crops had been blighted
Another wrong had to be righted
The warrior surged forth, unfazed by fear.

At their state, Gandhi was intensely pained
As blow upon blow on them was cruelly rained
The spirit vindictive
And the tone abrasive
Had to be strongly resisted, he maintained.

Gandhi with political workers planning Satyagraha in 1918

The crop was only a quarter of normal yield
Peasants were morose but their lips were sealed
Now came Gandhi on the scene
On his weapons he did lean
None can be governed without consent, he believed.

Their demand of suspension of annual revenue assessment
Filled the officials with intense resentment
Satyagraha had to be tried
Their conduct was undignified
Now, he plunged into moral rearmament.

On the brink of starvation the peasants did verge
But to get their due was the authorities' inhuman urge
To the occasion he did rise
Don't pay taxes, was his advice
The peasants obeyed giving rise to a great upsurge.

In the rampant environment of fear and dearth
Gandhi awakened them to a sense of worth
War was no excuse for oppression
It was his firm conviction
Was a renascent India now taking birth?

The peasants were trying to yank away shackles
In so doing, they had raised the authorities' hackles
But the man rare
Tried to rid them of fear
Amidst rampant jeers and scornful cackles!

Gandhi with CF Andrews

Along with Patel, he toured village after village
The pathetic condition filling him with outrage
Imparting lessons in simplicity
Warning them against incivility
The frail warrior felt strong with moral courage.

In full swing was the nonviolent battle
In retaliation, the officers seized their cattle
In disgust their lips curved
Penalty notices they served
When more people joined this unusual battle.

But the peasantry showed great fortitude
Even in the face of their callous attitude
In the dark they groped
For a light they hoped
His benevolent leadership filling them with gratitude.

The ruthless authorities were intensely sore
The no tax campaign lasted for months four
Now there was a compromise
The peasantry its joy couldn't disguise
This was a solution, without shedding gore.

No longer were misfortunes bewailed
On the government good sense prevailed
On the poor, the reins relaxed
The rich continued to be taxed
By the poor peasants this compromise was hailed.

By showing them the path of civil resistance
He had jolted them from their somnolence
This man of integrity
Infused a dignity
In the downtrodden with his moral influence.

Gandhi begins his nonviolent protest for India's freedom from British rule

Recruitment Drive

In 1918, war in Europe was raging with vigour
Any moment a crisis it would trigger
Fear of a German offensive
Made the British restive
They called a conference inviting the frail figure.

There he supported the resolution of recruitment
Filling many leaders with cringing embarrassment
A votary of nonviolence
Supporting recruitment made no sense
Was he deviating from his movement?

He again went to Kheda with a mission new
Into the peasants an energy to imbue
They listened in sullen silence
To the apostle of nonviolence
Senseless this language, and restless they grew.

They were filled with righteous ire
On this recruiting agent they poured fire
Rightly peeved
Gandhi still believed
In the fairness and justice of the Empire.

It was a stabilising force, was his firm conviction
Though he would always fight its oppression
Capable of generosity great
The Empire he couldn't berate
It would be folly to snap the British connection!

He exhorted the people with a zest new
But this Gandhi his friends hardly knew.
With wrath filled
To kill and be killed
This incomprehensible motto had takers few!

India would become a favoured partner in the Empire
Of singing paeans of its liberalism he didn't tire
This had no moral foundation
Andrews wanted an explanation
Unconvinced by this changed Inner Temple lawyer.

The response to his call was not enough
An unfazed Gandhi was made of unique stuff
Twenty miles a day he marched
With feet sore, and lips parched
Ignoring the snide remarks and strain tough.

In the earlier campaign in Kheda he was a hero
Now the untiring warrior felt like a zero
Accompanied by Patel
It was a sorry tale
When no warm welcome awaited the hero.

No carts were offered to them for transportation
All his pleas faced downright rejection.
His friends did panic
At this man quixotic
Whose views now seemed full of contradiction.

Not even hundred recruits did he find
Now, fate dealt a blow untimely and unkind
The hope he cherished
Alas, soon perished
For weeks seven, was bedridden this man kind.

Stubbornly he refused medical treatment
With growing panic was watched his derailment.
With health precarious
Death's designs nefarious
Appeared to be waiting for the opportune moment!

All around him the well-wishers were sad
Mystified by this illness so bad
Himself he cursed
Ashamed of being nursed
Harilal's children romped around their grand-dad!

Then came an ice-doctor like a ray of light
Ah, Gandhi was in a sorry plight
In great agony he lay
His body was wearing away
Having simply lost the spirit to fight.

On the bed lay the obstinate pacifist
Would he give into the ice-therapist?
The ashramites were on tenterhooks
Giving Gandhi anxious looks
Silently they stood, eyes on the ailing pacifist.

They watched the man who had their pleas defied
They craned their necks, stared round eyed.
The ice-therapist went near
Someone wiped a tear
Now, their joy they couldn't hide.

To ice-therapy had he really given his assent?
Into the hushed atmosphere there was excitement.
Into the emaciated figure
Was infused a fresh vigour
As he allowed the ice-therapist to experiment!

Now, in the distance a sinister storm rumbled
Gandhi's brow was intensely troubled
Would his people be harmed?
Gandhi was alarmed
He pricked his ears, and listened, brow troubled.

Rowlatt Bill

Out of the blue, now came a bombshell
On the public with evil force it fell.
This was the Rowlatt Bill
The public with wrath it did fill.
With righteous anger it started to swell.

To the ailing Gandhi this was a shock rude
To self- government an evil prelude
This duplicity he hated
He was agitated
Rebelliously stirring at this insensate attitude.

People scurried to him for consultation
How were they to fight this new legislation?
They were filled with dread
He had received stone for bread
On his bed he writhed in intense humiliation.

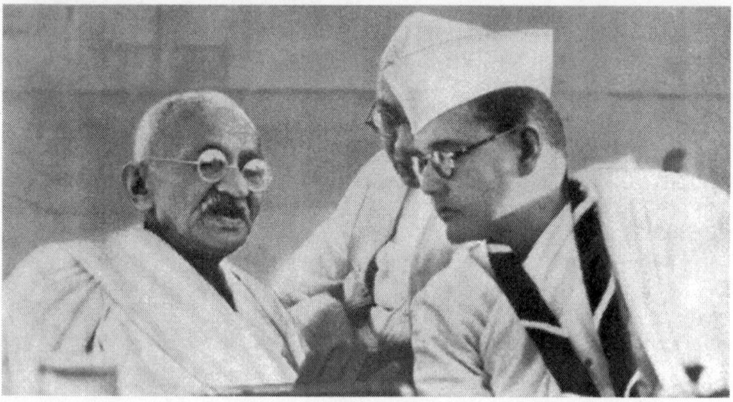

Gandhi with Gokhale (top); Gandhi with Subhash Chandra Bose (bottom)

The Bill provided an unfair deal
The people could be tried without a right of appeal
They bewailed
This freedom curtailed.
Was this a wound which would never heal?

In Delhi he listened to the debates on the Bill
Which proved to be an extremely bitter pill.
Though this draconian measure
Incurred rampant displeasure
No effort was made to withdraw it still.

Stunned by the authorities' callous indifference
And the poker-faced Viceroy's virulence
At his heart did claw
On18 March 1919 the Bill became law
He was struck dumb by this malfeasance.

Though still in the recuperation stage
Worry lines distorted his calm visage.
This act catalytic
Acted as a tonic
And hurtled him on the centre of the stage.

Through the nation ran a shock of high voltage
Ah, they were truly living in an unfair age.
This legislation oppressive
Of liberty was subversive
But the man did not lose his moral courage.

He traveled wide with the nonviolent message
In his speeches pouring out his outrage.
His face pale
And body frail
The warrior was not yet fifty years of age.

The Bill had caged them in their own house
From somnolence, the people he wanted to rouse.
On 19 March 1919
He appeared keen
By a general *hartal*, his country to arouse.

A voice had spoken to him in a dream
Hence he had decided upon this step extreme
He was in Madras in a meeting
The country was seething
To his host, Rajagopalachari he revealed his scheme.

The *hartal* would be accompanied by a fast
For twenty-four hours it would last.
The idea soon spread
Filling the authorities with dread
In a common bond the multitudes it cast.

Delhi observed it on 30th March, the rest on 6th April.
When the country came to a standstill.
Gandhi was pleasantly surprised
The authorities' wrath ill-disguised
At this enthusiasm which was a bitter pill.

Swami Shraddhanand was sent an invitation
To speak at Jama Masjid in a revolutionary action.
In orange robes attired
With a passion fired
In Chandni Chowk, later he led a huge procession.

Suddenly on the scene, Gurkha troops emerged.
With fervour rare, onward the procession surged.
The portents were not good.
In a belligerent mood
The troops wanted the rally violently purged.

In a show of bravado, his breast he bared.
To shoot him first, the troops he dared.
Filled with great ire
They opened fire
For the loss of lives they hardly cared!

In Bombay it was marked under Gandhi's supervision.
On 6 April, normal business followed a suspension.
On the Chowpatti beach
People did reach
The authorities gaped in incomprehension.

In the evening, in a slow moving car
In defiance of the ban, they went far.
In this unusual ride
Sarojini sat by his side
Selling his banned books in an act bizarre.

Ten rupees were paid for books of annas four
At this rebel, the authorities were sore.
Though with anger they burned
A blind eye they turned
Wondering what for them was further in store.

Gandhi was aghast at the forces of violence
Lying dormant among the people of sense.
In a mood gray
On 7th April he left Bombay
For Delhi where the situation was tense.

The violence in Delhi and Punjab on his brain
At Palwal on 9th April, he was pulled off the train.
On this railway station small
Gandhi was filled with gall
Why, from violence people could not refrain.

On a cot he lay guarded by sepoys four
While the raging violence at his heart tore.
He felt as if on the rack
To Bombay he was sent back
In indignation people did roar!

Here, by jubilant crowds he was greeted
Like a long-lost celebrity he was treated
Meetings he addressed
While people jostled and pressed
Soon the atmosphere with official wrath heated.

In a meeting, he had spoken only a words few
When the mounted police appeared, as if on cue.
Vindictively they charged
Into the crowd they barged
Iron-tipped lathis they swung, bitter the brew!

Blindly through the mob, lancers cut their way
While the crowd gaped in utter dismay.
Utterly stunned, they cursed
But soon dispersed.
To the Commissioner's office Gandhi stormed his way.

Wrathfully to the Commissioner he complained
Crowds were uncontrolled, the Commissioner explained.
That he didn't doubt Gandhi's intention
This he did clearly mention
From resorting to violence, people couldn't be refrained.

Beyond his comprehension was his language
His was not the language of a savage
In love he believed
The British were peeved
When six hundred people in Bombay signed the pledge.

With the skeptics Gandhi had no desire to argue
The British were afraid of this weapon new.
They would finally yield
Gandhi strongly believed
If to this Satyagraha pledge, the people were true.

A knife thrust couldn't have pained him more
At the senseless gore, his heart was sore.
At the campaign stained
He was intensely pained
His foes gloated at the point they did score!

To Ahmedabad he went, it was under martial law
He was aghast at the rampant violence he saw.
Shops were plundered
Where had he blundered?
Did his movement have some inherent flaw?

In scathing tones, the violence he did criticize
His feelings, he made no effort to disguise
He would now go on a fast
For seventy-two hours it would last
Rampant speculation was now on the rise.

From Sabarmati, Gandhi went to Nadiad
A town in Kheda, twenty-nine miles from Ahmedabad.
Violence was spreading fast
At the 'Himalayan miscalculation' aghast
Ruefully he told the people at Nadiad.

The skeptics said their stand had been vindicated
The campaign had failed as they had indicated.
The Satyagraha campaign
Had given him immense pain
On 18th April he called off the campaign ill-fated.

In civil disobedience people should be trained
A distraught Gandhi now emphatically maintained.
Critics scoffed
And derisively laughed
That decisive victory over him they had gained.

Love he wanted to establish over force
To sublimity craving to restore moral force.
Was this man energetic
Taking a pause strategic
To reconsider the feasibility of this difficult course?

In the meantime, Punjab balefully boiled
Soon horrendous incidents uncoiled.
There occurred a blast
Leaving the people aghast
With a turbulence rare, the waters roiled.

Brigadier General Dyer held command of the force
In Amritsar, heading towards a gruesome course.
For glory he did thirst
And as his order first
Banned mass meetings, prelude to the use of force.

Jallianwala Bagh

In Jallianwala Bagh people were in festive mood
On 13th April 1919, in ambush, lay a shock rude.
On that Baisakhi day ill-fated
6,000 people had congregated
Ignorant of the dubious ways for which Dyer stood.

With his war record, his ambitions did soar
With premature glee, this Irishman did roar.
With anger he burned
When he learned
That a meeting had been called at half-past four!

The orders had reached few areas of the city
Laying the ground for a reprehensible atrocity.
At this defiance deliberate
He shook with wrath great
Unleashing a demonic power of great velocity.

Into the garden now stormed Brigadier General Dyer
With a disregard brutal ordered his troops to fire.
In the rush pell-mell
Many stumbled and fell
Ecstatic with glee, Dyer's men continued to fire.

Many over a five foot wall tried to leap
In panic wild, women started to weep.
Some into a well jumped
Others in horror slumped.
Stealthy Death, towards them started to sweep.

Now, over this bloody finale the man gloated.
With this accomplishment, he now felt bloated.
With his armoured might
Amritsar now in a sorry plight
With a victorious swagger, he now floated.

Heartlessly, he defended the indefensible deed
Humanity was definitely not his creed
For this heinous offence
There could be no defense
But, this man belonged to a savage breed.

Force is the language understood by the Asiatic
Was the vile plea for this crime barbaric.
Gandhi filled with fury
At Dyer's butchery
Resolved not to cooperate with this government satanic.

Now, it was time for further punishment
The Asiatic had no right to show resentment.
Beaten and humiliated
Flogged and intimidated
In every way, on them was their ire vent.

Thunderstruck was the country at this gore
Ah—its heart had been pierced to the core.
Guilty of a gross monstrosity
The Empire lost its credibility
India gave vent to a heart wrenching roar!

With cruelty, was massacred an innocent throng
But in this action, Dyer found nothing wrong.
Remarked the man unfair
With insanely pompous air
That he only wanted to shoot well and strong!

On 10th April, Ms Sherwood was attacked
For this act, now vengeance he wrecked.
Filled with gall
He made people crawl
Where this headmistress of a school was attacked!

After two days, martial law he proclaimed
As the Asiatic had forcefully to be tamed.
Followed a strict censorship
Hardship upon hardship
The people had to be crushed, he claimed.

Gandhi with Nehru and Patel (top); Gandhi with Rajagopalachari planning non-cooperation movements (bottom)

Non-cooperation

Reeling under intense humiliation
No longer would they tolerate the repression
Boycott was the watchword now
No longer would they cower and bow
In June, Khilafat movement approved non-cooperation.

By this rampant ill will and oppression appalled
A session of the Congress in Calcutta was called
In September 1920 the resolution stressed
Khilafat and Punjab wrongs had to be redressed
No longer could they be stalled.

The national honour would be vindicated
Only by nonviolent non-cooperation, it indicated
By Lala Lajpat Rai presided
Many, this resolution derided
The programme was adopted, and victory celebrated.

It would unleash anarchy, the critics saw red
'It is foolish', a circular of 4th September 1920 said.
It was their surmise
That noninterference was wise
So, in the circumstances, cautious their tread.

Repression would make them martyrs to the cause.
It was advisable to watch and pause
So in this clime
They bided their time
To arrest him for an offence under the laws.

The annual session in Nagpur followed now.
Despite internal opposition, he did not bow.
With exemplary dignity
Emphasized the futility
Of violence, reinforcing the sublimity of love.

The Congress now needed to be mass based
Not a forum by vacuous oratory debased
It had to be refashioned
He said in tones impassioned
A representative character it now embraced.

No longer the preserve of the upper classes
Its doors were flung open to the masses.
Of violence purged
Onward the people surged
On the streets converged men, women and lasses.

Imbued with vigour they could walk many a mile
Under Gandhi, who for twenty-three years was in exile
With his simplicity and humility
Striking a chord in India's humanity
This half-naked figure had acquired a unique style.

Into active soldiers, armchair politicians turned
Now with an intense ardour they burned
Leaders anglicised
Now energised
Becoming servants of society, comforts they spurned.

Many gave up their careers under his leadership
Resolving to brave every roadblock and hardship
They headed toward jail
Buoyed by the man frail
Undeterred by flogging, or the crack of a whip.

Now in the darkness emerged a shining star
Moti Lal Nehru gave up practice at Allahabad bar
He had never enjoyed life better
To Gandhi he wrote in a letter
Shorn of lucre, strengthened by a moral power.

Life became meaningful on the difficult terrain
By renouncing their comforts, they had much to gain
With a smile on cracked lips
Many a teenager braved the whips
Deriving immense pleasure from the inflicted pain.

In a nation enslaved, he behaved like a free man
To him for counsel many confused ones ran.
Non-cooperation had an instant appeal
Its simplicity had the power to heal
Where to start, the horizon he started to scan.

Convinced that one day he would wring repentance
Be granted a fuller measure of independence.
With the weapons in his armoury
He would convert his adversary
This optimistic man brimmed over with confidence.

On 2nd April 1921, Lord Reading became Viceroy
His mind whirring with a list of tactics to employ.
Gandhi was in the fray
Whom he met in May
For him, Fabian tactics would be the ploy.

Between them there were meetings six
On many topics of an eclectic mix
He confessed he was thrilled
And with awe filled
But regarding his politics in a total fix.

The nationalist tide was ebbing, they thought
Actually the atmosphere was getting hot.
The popular discontent
Caused embarrassment
The authorities on the wrong foot were caught.

The Prince of Wales landed in Bombay
On 7th November 1921, for them a grey day.
The non-cooperators abstained
The government was pained
And Gandhi from the ceremonies kept away.

The Prince was greeted by brooding silence
For the authorities this was planned impertinence
The non-cooperators all afire
On the supporters vented their ire
Wrathful the authorities at this malevolence.

In utter indignation their arms they flailed
Bent on drastic action thousands they jailed.
Meetings were dispersed
Non-cooperators were cursed
Enraged at their programmes being derailed.

The Congress met in December nineteen twenty-one
To deliberate on what was to be done
The struggle had to be intensified
The unjust laws to be defied
Another battle had to be won without a gun.

The whole of India had to be liberated
No longer could it remain mutilated
But any note of discord
Gandhi could ill afford
In somber tones this he indicated.

For Chelmsford, the most foolish of all schemes
For Gandhi, a compendium of his dreams
The weapon of the brave
Through which he did crave
To realise freedom supported by his non- violent teams.

Towards a self-disciplined Bardoli his eyes turned
A policy of senseless gore he had always spurned
He would never go wrong
With his ammunition strong
Ignorant of the fire that in his followers burned.

Chauri Chaura

On 1st February 1922, to Reading, he wrote a letter
Before plunging head-long into the stormy weather.
To him he communicated
The step that he contemplated
But the letter was treated with contempt utter.

Chauri Chaura was catapulted on centrestage
On 5th February 1922, the scene of an outrage.
A procession passed the police station
A matter of great consternation
Followed this, resulting in a brutal carnage.

As the police station the procession neared
At the stragglers the constables jeered
On a wave of indignation astride
They retaliated in anger wild
None was amused, when violence its head reared.

People fleeing from police during the Chauri Chaura agitation

The soup overflowed as the cauldron bubbled
Every brow was now intensely troubled
At the police station people converged
In their hearts a patriotic fervour surged
Towards the constables they raced, their blood curdled.

To escape their wrath in the station they found shelter
After them ran the indignant crowd helter skelter
With fists upraised
Slogans they raised
Racing towards the station where they had found shelter.

They stumbled on in wrath unrestrained
At the injustice, indignantly they complained
Shouting in tones incisive
And wrath abrasive
Till their throats pained and arms complained.

Twenty-thousand surrounded the police station
Minds churning with malevolent intention
Seething at this action unfair
They wrung their hands in despair
Now bent on a path of violent destruction.

In a frenzy, they set fire to the police station
Which soon suffered a fiery annihilation
The flames leapt
Into the station they crept
Singeing policemen cowering there in desperation.

People watched with eyes horror filled
Some in huddled knots stood, their blood chilled
More than twenty policemen fell to the fire
The straits indeed were dire
In this act, revenge on the streets had spilled.

On the uncharted ocean he had sailed
The lurking dangers he now bewailed
The cauldron bubbled
In pain he doubled
Had his experiment of nonviolence failed?

No provocation can justify murder, he exclaimed.
For the protestors' crime, himself he blamed.
He went on a fast
For five days which did last
For a suspension of the campaign he aimed.

The movement faded and detractors jeered.
No choice but to call it off, they sneered.
Deeply anguished
His values most cherished
Had got burnt in this fire, so weird.

Let foes gloat in our humiliation, he intoned.
Though, for the loss of sanity he mourned
In nonviolence, he maintained
The resisters had to be trained
In self-restraint, their skills to be honed.

The pros and cons of his arrest were debated.
Said some, it was high time he was incarcerated
On a dilemma perched
In the legal jungle ways they searched
Of arresting one, who a disturbance had created.

After procrastination, on 10th March1922
In an important decision long overdue
He was suddenly no longer free
They imprisoned this man of fifty-three.
For writing three articles, in a spirit true.

To the inmates of the ashram he bid adieu
After hearing the song of the Vaishnav true
The man frail
Was driven to jail
Mulling over what to do in the environment new.

Gandhi in jail

Imprisonment

Sedition was their creed, said the man of integrity
In the first article: 'Tampering with loyalty'.
On 19 September 1921
Fearlessly wrote this son
The government was shocked at his sheer audacity.

On December 1921, 'A puzzle and its solution'
He wrote in answer to the rampant confusion
The government was irked
But Gandhi felt perked
For fighting all evils his weapon non-cooperation.

'Shaking the manes', was his article third
With vehemence rare was laced each word.
It was his ardent wish
To fight to the finish
Had the man a hornet's nest stirred?

With the wine of power and plunder intoxicated.
The Empire had exhibited brute force, he stated
Toward the end of February
In this article inflammatory
Strongly, the British Empire he berated.

On 18th March 1922, the great trial took place
Not a frown flitted across his calm face
Offering himself for penalty
He pleaded guilty
Wreathed in smiles, dignified his grace.

The dhoti-clad figure now faced judge Broomfield
With a sincere eloquence his lips were now unsealed
He did not mouth any platitude
Somber his attitude
The courteous judge the gavel did not wield.

Unmarked by ill will, malice or dread
The trial lasted for minutes hundred
On trial a leader great
There was no hidden bait
'I could not have expected greater courtesy.'

Though he had no grudge against any administrator
He had turned into a non-cooperator
This man of rectitude
Unwilling to prolong India's servitude
Had thus become a nonviolent agitator.

In his armoury, nonviolence an effective tool
To bring an end to unjust British rule
It was his conclusion
That prevalent exploitation
Could be confronted with this impeccable tool.

To all the charges Gandhi pleaded guilty
Emphasising the government's evil influence in totality
Neither indulging in semantic jugglery
Nor resorting to specious sophistry
His case he stated with heart-warming simplicity.

To agricultural resources, spinning was a supplement
The people wove and spun before the British advent
Through the British heartlessness
India had sunk into lifelessness
This pathetic state of affairs Gandhi did lament.

He was sentenced to six years simple imprisonment
The judge beamed while paying him a compliment
He would be pleased
If he was released
Or term reduced by the repentant government.

In the Yervada prison, he did not feel insecure
The inconveniences he was ready to endure
In this experience new
There were pinpricks few
Life in Yervada was like an 'arrest cure'.

In Kipling's *Barrack Room Ballads*, Goethe's *Faust*
The passionate bibliophile was absolutely lost
Bernard Shaw's *Man and Superman*
Awed this voracious man
For sedition, jail life was not a heavy cost!

Henry James' *The Varieties of Religious Experience*
To him made immense sense
And Buckle's *History of Civilization*
Filled him with admiration
Surrounded by books, he felt no longer tense.

Of Gibbon's *Decline and fall of the Roman Empire*
He read on and he could never tire
Wells' *Outline of History*
Unraveled many a mystery
This voyage into the unknown set him afire.

Appendicitis found him outside the Sasoon hospital door
In Poona, in January nineteen twenty four
A weird situation they faced
When on the operating table placed
The lights went off making Maddock sore.

In the light of a torch he was operated
At the success of the operation everyone elated.
About his condition concerned
The tables now turned
His immediate release was frantically debated.

On 5 February 1924, he was released
But Gandhi was not at all pleased
Not a reason valid
What if he looked pallid
With the dissensions in the Congress utterly displeased.

For recuperation he was shifted to Juhu,
Where visited CR Das and Motilal Nehru
In this sea side resort
His blessings they sought
With every waking moment pensive he grew.

The policy of obstruction from within they deliberated
It was through boycott that India could be liberated
It was his surmise
That council entry was unwise
With these Swarajists he vociferously remonstrated.

The Swaraj Party now held centrestage
During his absence, in the clime was a change.
Communal harmony had suffered a blow
Constructive programme was slow
The mutual bickering filled him with outrage.

His faith was shaken and he lost sleep
Realising that nonviolence was skin deep
At a Congress meeting in June 1924
He wanted to run out of the door
When Khadi was opposed, composure he couldn't keep.

At the Belgaum Congress in December1924
In a tone which was weary and sore
His ire ill disguised
Self-sacrifice he emphasised
The antagonism pierced his heart to the core.

He lamented the mess into which they had slipped
The constructive programme had dipped
In the atmosphere volatile
Differences he wanted to reconcile
Trying to yank away the misgivings by which gripped.

Demoralised, now from the political scene he retired
Unable to endure the mess into which India was mired
His disillusionment he did not mask
Addressing himself to an important task
With redoubled vigour, the frail figure was fired.

Through the countryside he travelled by bullock cart
On the treacherous terrain, healing many a heart
Thousands to him flocked
At the deification he baulked
Of his programme, spinning an important part.

The indomitable crusader did not stumble or totter
Moving through bramble and stinking water
Shunning luxurious travel
And did not cavil
Even when the weather grew sultry and hotter.

On his *charkha* obsession, British heaped ridicule
He made it the symbol of defiance to foreign rule.
He appealed to the idle man
And the famished woman
To spin away to freedom, he was no fool.

For the widow and the farmer undernourished
Many an ardent dream he cherished.
He said with great feeling
That with its touch healing
India would no longer remain unflourished.

It would forge links between town and village
Freeing India from a suffocating bondage
Was his conviction strong
But some thought it wrong
That it should be a cult, filling them with rage.

It would bring monotony, Tagore complained
Spin only for half an hour, he explained.
In answer to India's poverty
Said the man of morality
Anguished by the ills to which they were chained.

In 1925, he went to Central India and Kathiawar
Then onward to Bengal, Travancore and Malabar
He travelled a lot
Even when it was hot
Though with dangers fraught, he had to go far.

For him nineteen twenty-six was a year of silence
Finding solace in Sabarmati Ashram's benevolence
For him Khadi and fasting
Had an interest lasting
Along with his policy of nonviolence.

Early in 1927, his touring he resumed with zest
The pilgrim believed he had taken enough rest
Thirty meetings a week and six a day
Was no child's play
But the tireless pilgrim knew what was best.

Now his wanderings started taking their toll
Would he have to quit pursuing his goal?
His eyes were blurred
And his head whirled
Undeterred by ill health he played his role.

From apathy the people he unshackled
On the difficult path many problems he tackled.
India was rising from slumber deep
No longer gripped by a comatose sleep
To orthodoxy some continued to be shackled.

He was advised rest in a place cool
He went to Mysore, events started to unspool.
By May 1927, he felt better
Now nothing could deter
The man, rest having acted as fuel.

After twenty months in Europe, Nehru returned
About the atmosphere new things he learned.
India brimmed with energy suppressed
And was highly impressed
That the quiescent India with a fire burned.

Latent energy was harnessed amid weather rough.
The government reeled under a time tough.
Agrarian discontent raised its head
At this government saw red
No longer apathetic, people had waited enough.

SIMON, GO BACK

Simon Commission

For the British ambiguous was the clime
They appointed a commission two years before time.
Although guided
By what the Act of 1919 provided
The Indians remained unimpressed by its reason prime.

Birkenhead appointed this commission new
This seven-member commission had takers few
Filled with apprehension
Against this all-White commission
A resolution passed by sixty-eight votes to sixty-two.

It reached Bombay to windows shuttered.
In ire unprecedented the authorities muttered
The audacity they could not bear
As cries of 'Simon go back', rent the air
Like a wounded bird their wings they now fluttered.

On October 30, 1928 in Lahore
Lajpat Rai let out an impassioned roar.
Lathi blows fell on his chest
For the Indians a cruel test
On 17 November 1928, the lion was no more.

To the lathi blows he had fallen victim
The country watched in horror grim
In hearts this did trigger
A new passion and vigour
The sun in the eastern horizon was dim.

For the British government no hope glimmered
In people righteous indignation simmered
Stricter became the government attitude
To the people giving no latitude
For whom hope in the horizon shimmered.

A number of parties now came together
To brave this stormy weather
At this challenge hurled
The authorities' lips curled
Had they reached the end of the tether?

To a new movement he was now geared
Which was surely no impracticality weird.
If their demand was not heeded
And dominion status not conceded
Towards this goal the country would be steered.

The ball was now in the court of the opponent
The next move now lay with the government.
He was again on his way
Many more evils to slay
Before hitting the government with a new movement.

Onward progressed the pilgrim, deterred not a bit.
The meager clothed figure was spiritually fit.
Give up sloth
Boycott foreign cloth.
Implored he with his unique brand of wit.

At the momentous Congress session in Lahore
In December 1929 revolutionary things were in store.
To make him the president inclined
But he shrewdly declined
To Jawaharlal Nehru he now passed the oar.

Now this forty-year-old emerged as his heir
With many new expectations, crisp was the air.
A rare emotional affinity
And a mutual loyalty
Had strengthened this bond of affection rare.

In a move immensely significant and great
'Purna swaraj' was declared as the goal ultimate.
A challenge was hurled
When the tricolor was unfurled
At midnight on 31 December 1929, on this date.

On 26 January 1930, Independence Day was celebrated
The effects of this the British fervently deliberated.
This fake independence
To them made no sense
In inchoate rage, the rulers expostulated.

For another movement the country was ripe
Involving people of every hue and stripe
So he was rearing to go
To render another blow
With a crusade which was one of its type.

Dandi March

Now he started a March historic
Stirring peoples' imagination in a move dramatic
Which left a mark
And ignited a spark
Becoming a wild fire in an event chaotic!

The salt tax was unjust was the Indian standpoint.
On 2 March, to the Viceroy Gandhi wrote his viewpoint.
Notifying his intention
To break it, he did mention.
The government failed to see the point.

By boiling water no Empire had been unseated
With scorn contemptuous, was his plan treated.
A project fantastic
By a man quixotic
What followed none could have anticipated!

Lord Irwin sent a curt four-line acknowledgment
Stating that his action, would be an infringement.
'On bended knees I asked for bread
And I have received stone instead!'
Exclaimed Gandhi in absolute resentment.

The place selected for law-breaking was Dandi.
Filled with an enthusiasm rare was Gandhi.
From his ashram at Ahmedabad
On 12 March 1930, he started with a band
Of seventy-eight ashramites towards Dandi.

With a step firm and love for his land
Onward marched the warrior staff in hand.
Was he a maverick
Or simply eccentric?
His tactics the English unable to understand.

The Indians with sheer excitement bubbled
The brow of the administrators was troubled.
Filled with dread
At the trouble ahead
With the burden of anxiety their backs doubled.

To Dandi, a seaside village in Gujarat
Walked they with a flutter in many a heart.
They carried no gun
Trudging miles two hundred and forty-one
On 5th April he reached this village in Gujarat.

First day's march ended, thirteen miles from Ahmedabad
Gandhi's frailty, couldn't the March retard.
This man of sixty- one
Many a wrong had undone
In the past, never yearning for any award.

Putting the people under his spell hypnotic
By addressing many a meeting public
This man of great integrity
Appeared moving almost in surreality
Exhorting people to disloyalty, was he quixotic?

They traversed dirt roads from village to village
Headmen giving up their posts, caused government rage.
Even Kasturba Gandhi
In a sari of orange Khadi
Marched on with the warriors on this pilgrimage.

He thought that the youth was delicate
Some were tired, Gandhi a walker first rate.
No trouble had he in walking
With the people gawking
With his strides the weaklings he did berate!

The Nehrus met him at Jambusar
Walking a little distance with this star.
Exhorted by the little figure
Women picketed shops of liquour
He said that for them Dandi was Haridwar.

Sacrifices were many, a war had to be won.
Motilal Nehru gifted his house, Anand Bhavan.
The man unarmed walked
Rampant enthusiasm sparked
Was a new nation really about to be born?

The government guffawed in amusement
The man in loin cloth, ignoring the government
Walked on towards his destination
Smiling at their derision
Reflecting the glow of enhanced excitement.

At his fixation with salt, the cynics jeered.
The magician walked on, the onlookers cheered.
Followed by a human tide
Some watched from the roadside
As the pilgrims progressed, the destination neared.

On 6th April, he walked to the beach
Yearning with a zest to reach the beach.
To tackle the foe
The figure bent low
Hailed by everyone converged on the beach.

The wizard, bent low only to soar high.
Picking up a lump of salt, he gave the lie
To the sceptics' view
That his fad new
Of choosing salt would be a vacuous cry.

Now, as one man, rose the entire country
To salute this son in unrestrained glee
Who had performed a conjurer's trick
A lump of salt when he bent down to pick
He had rendered his countrymen free.

The world gaped in incredulity
At these actions sheathed in morality.
People brazenly indolent
No more somnolent
Rejoicing in this new-found dignity!

In a direction new, his country he did gear
Free from manacled impotence and fear
Liberated from age-old shackles
Ignoring the contemptuous cackles
Freedom from unjust servitude was now near.

A pinch of salt had thrown it off gear
The so-called powers now cowered in fear.
How they did hate
This upsurge great.
Minds churning with new tactics of generating fear.

They found the ground slipping under their feet
Afraid they would soon lose their imperial seat.
This act of defiance symbolic
Had made the situation catastrophic
Now, severe brutalities they started to mete.

They lost sleep over this arm-less insurrection
Where salt was made by people of every section.
Men and women, young and old
Both the meek and the bold
Made salt, filling them with frustration.

Contraband salt was now openly sold
Robust became their pitch, and they grew bold.
To the skies their zest leapt
The government out of its depth.
The cheap salt having become almost gold.

The high and mighty government was in a fix.
Jawaharlal Nehru was sentenced for months six
JM Sengupta, the Calcutta Mayor
At a meeting read seditious literature
And earned sentence for months six!

Intellectuals, students, both male and female
The rich and the poor, the healthy and the frail
The motley crowd
In batches proud
Were marched off to jail without fail.

Jolted out of slumber, the country felt rejuvenated
With a reckless abandon, women demonstrated.
Horrified by this agitation rare
The government wrung its hands in despair
When literature on salt production was distributed.

In 1919, even in the face of horrifying cruelty
Gandhi's voice had pleaded for sanity
The violence in 1922
Had made Gandhi rue
So, when beaten, they refrained from insanity.

On 4th May 1930, slept he on a cot
Probably dreaming of stemming the pernicious rot.
His camp was at Karadi,
Three miles from Dandi
By his side slept the pilgrims, tired a lot.

In the pitch dark, footsteps were heard.
On the tree, in panic fluttered a bird.
It screeched its displeasure
At the ashramites' discomfiture
Who looked around, as more steps were heard.

There was commotion in the leafy compound
One sound followed another strange sound.
Who were these nocturnal intruders
Were they some lost marauders?
Who, in the compound had some treasure found?

In Gandhi's face someone shone a flashlight.
Nothing could be more ridiculous than the sight
Of a half-naked Gandhi
In a village in Dandi
Confronted by a heavily armed party at midnight!

The British DM of Surat, Indian officers two
With thirty policemen in the entourage too.
'Do you want me?' asked Gandhi
At the dead of night in Karadi
The heavily armed visitors were quite a few.

'Are you Gandhi?' The magistrate asked
Gandhi looked around, expression masked.
'I have come to arrest you', said the magistrate.
Was this another trap being laid by fate?
'Will I get time for ablutions', Gandhi asked ?

Gandhi, by now, was out of bed
The pilgrims had crowded around the shed.
He cleaned his teeth few
Getting ready for his home new
He wanted some time for prayers, he said.

Pandit Khare recited the hymn, 'Vaishnavjana'
For the warrior fighting without a gun.
Gandhi was now arrested
Alas, the pilgrim had not rested.
At 1:10 am, he was driven to Yervada Prison.

To raid Dharsana salt works was his ambition
To the Viceroy, in a letter he did mention
Before he could implement the plan
The government had another plan
He was arrested before he could carry out his intention.

Hartals and strikes followed Gandhi's internment
All over India, people were filled with resentment
There were resignations enmasse
The government had come to a sorry pass
The west had also become sympathetic—a predicament!

Now, Abbas Tyabji took Gandhi's place
The show must go on keeping up its pace
But he was also arrested
And the opportunity from his hands wrested
By a lady who came as a saving grace!

Now, they marched without their main leader
Gandhi their chief inspirer and motivator
Was in Yervada jail
But the Satyagrahis didn't fail
To carry out his plan under this new leader!

Sarojini Naidu, was their leader new
With her followers 2,500, not few
With Imam Sahib's assistance
On their path of recalcitrance
Onwards marched the pilgrims in manner true.

Dharsana Salt Depot was 150 miles north of Bombay
But, for the ebullient group, this was child's play.
Not to raise a hand
She told the committed band
Forward marched the warriors, north of Bombay.

Thus motivated by India's brave daughter
Not browbeaten by the police, they didn't falter
None was a coward
Towards the salt pans they moved forward
Which were surrounded by ditches filled with water.

Gandhi's son, Manilal, was in the forefront
They reached the pans, ready to bear the brunt
There was great bodily harm
To ward off the blows none raised an arm
No publicity stunt, but vicious became the hunt.

On skulls, blows fell with lathis steel-shod
The onlookers groaned, invoking their god
None shed a tear
Or wavered in fear
They were marching for a cause in the name of the Lord.

Steadily they moved on, heads high
In silence eloquent, they walked, without a sigh.
Onward they marched
With lips parched
Exhausted and foot sore, but not afraid to die!

The police was enraged by the moral doggedness
Of the disciples of this man of a rare kindness
Organised nonviolence
Can check violence
His iron will cloaked in a feathery softness.

The powerful were gripped in powerlessness
In rage impotent, they seethed at their helplessness
Suffering indignity upon cruel indignity
Some pilgrims died with great dignity
While the living spread gory mindlessness!

Now, into the ditches were the pilgrims thrown
Brutally struck with lathis, they did groan.
Profusely they bled
To the hospital they were led
On their parched lips a silent moan.

A frail toothless man, five feet five in height
Had shown the world that he could bite
With a rare moral vigour
The short figure
Had defeated England morally, and risen in height!

With her moral tenacity, India was now invincible
In frustration, the government its nails did nibble
It felt embarrassed
And very harassed
To imprison the pilgrims and their leader feeble.

Lord Irwin's administration had screeched to a halt
For which, obviously Gandhi was at fault
Unrest was on the mount
And they had lost count
Of warriors injured, those arrested for making salt!

In a dilemma severe, the situation they did hate
But with the peaceful rebel they had to negotiate
So to the jail they sent
A newspaper correspondent
With the intention of attending to matters immediate.

George Slocombe, a reporter for the *Daily Herald*
In jail an interview with Gandhi held
In this conversation
The terms of negotiation
He gave to Slocombe of *Daily Herald.*

Now arrived Jayakar and Sapru to jail.
Alas in their mission they did fail
Gandhi couldn't take a decision
Before a consultation
With the CWC, its stalwarts were brought to jail.

From their jail in United Provinces to his prison
Were transported the Nehrus, father and son.
Also confined in Gandhi's jail
Were Sarojini and Patel
Irwin brought them for a discussion in the prison.

By boiling water no emperor has been unseated.
With contempt was Gandhi's plan treated
A project fantastic
By a man quixotic
Was the view, what followed was not anticipated.

With venom rampant, it was a turbulent season
'We will have no truck with treason.'
Winston Churchill vowed
But the warriors unbowed
Resolved to do and die, strong their reason.

The discussions lasted for two days
But they proved to be a wild goose chase!
They were absolutely unable
To bridge the gulf unbridgeable
Between the British and Congress, in this phase!

Gandhi-Irwin Pact

Within a week now followed the release
Of Gandhi and others in a bid to appease
And to remove stumbling blocks
Prior to Gandhi-Irwin talks
So, this opportunity they wanted to seize.

The stage was set, for talks between the statesmen
In the Viceroy's dazzling palace, met two men.
Due to domestic opposition
There could be no substantial concession
For the talks that on 17 February 1931 began.

To Churchill the Indians were of poor quality
He was repelled by their cheeky audacity.
For him it was nauseating
And also humiliating
That a fakir should negotiate on the basis of equality!

Gandhi and Lord Irwin

The fragile fakir sat in the ornate study
Of the Viceroy whose face was ruddy.
Small, wizened and emaciated
Keen interest he generated
With his frail body which was morally sturdy.

Meagerly clad in his loin cloth it was no satire
On the gigantic figure in his imperial attire.
Swathed in integrity
His powerful personality
More than made up for the paucity of his attire!

With him he talked without a confrontational air
In the frail figure finding a man rare
Utterly at ease and supremely confident
Sat Gandhi in the palace resplendent
Conferring with the lanky aristocratic heir.

The six feet five inch man, heir to an estate wide
The poorly clad, five foot five figure, did not deride.
With trust and sincerity
And immense capability
In hammering out a truce both sincerely tried.

It was an affair long where nerves jangled
While the two men talked and wrangled
The weather rough
The bargaining tough
Before them a task to disentangle the mess tangled!

Intermittently they conferred, overcoming many a hardship
Thus emerged a basis for a new relationship
On 4 March 1931, through efforts combined
The pact was finally signed
Gandhi hoped that permanent would be this new friendship.

Churchill spewed venom at this man veracious
At Indian lawyers, fanatics, merchants rapacious.
To his intense ire
The mighty British Empire
Was now at the mercy of this fakir seditious!

Some concessions were given with reluctance
Which, alas, did not carry much substance
But for Gandhi, the principle of equality
Extracted from the British polity
Was significant, filling him with exuberance.

The Congress would call off Civil Disobedience
Attend the second Round Table Conference
It was pleased
That prisoners would be released
On issues many, irked by governmental intransigence.

India does not want to be nursed like a sickly child
Said Gandhi on 5th March, in a tone not mild
It wanted nothing less
Than complete independence
With sops it would no longer be beguiled.

The pact was subjected to severe criticism
For many, nothing but sheer sentimentalism.
But he held his ground
A new basis he had found
Amply fortified to tackle this rampant cynicism.

Not to aim at the foe's physical elimination
This he believed with an unusual passion.
Convinced about this Satyagraha logic
To return to the battle he was emphatic
If government was guilty of its violation.

No power could keep India in bondage
She would be free when she came of age
He stuck to his technique
Filling many with pique
And they lashed out in righteous outrage.

After the pact was signed, he received an ovation
Surprising Bose at this universal adulation.
Soon complaints of non-fulfillment
Against the government
Lead to another round of hectic negotiation.

In Bengal and Bombay after months few
The recurrence of terrorist activities Gandhi did rue.
The path of the gun
Had been overdone
The value of nonviolence he wanted to imbue.

In April, Gandhi bid farewell to Irwin in Bombay
Lord Willingdon was the new Viceroy in the fray
Breaches of the pact
Had to be dealt with tact
He conveyed to the Viceroy, in a mood gray.

This was followed by a resumption of negotiation
Which did not lack recrimination
A compromise sound
Was mutually found
This lessened somewhat the rampant apprehension.

Second Round Table Conference

Complaints would be tackled, it was relief immense
He would participate in second Round Table Conference
As the Congress' sole delegate
This was a step great
Like a ray peeping from behind clouds dense.

He reached Bombay in a train from Simla to Kalka
On 29th August 1931 in the SS Rajputana.
Leaving his motherland
He sailed for England
Accompanied by Sarojini Naidu, Mirabehn, and Malviya.

Mahadev Desai, Payare Lal and Devdas were there
But his mood bordered on utter despair.
The horizon appeared black
Empty-handed he would be back
He dared to hope, not bogged down by undue care.

Gandhi being welcomed in England

In the ship, he plied the spinning wheel
For the boisterous children, a fascinating deal.
At Marseilles, by Madeline Rolland he was greeted
By French students, courteously treated.
At this warmth, his joy he couldn't conceal.

On 12th September 1931 he reached London
Where many important tasks had to be done
The rich offered their hospitality
But he turned down this opportunity
Of living in big houses in the heart of London.

For, his heart was with his own kind
He knew immense joy he would find
Among the common folks
Though his friends did coax
He stayed with Muriel Lester, the pacifist kind.

Born to wealth, poverty she had embraced.
Founding Kingsley Hall, where a cell he graced.
To the chagrin of the rest
He stayed as Lester's guest
Surrounded by children's chatter with affection laced.

Through puddles he splashed barefoot
The photographers after him ran to shoot
This celebrity tall
Who in loin cloth and shawl
Bobbed up and down streets in joy absolute.

When a reporter, about his dress answer did seek
This witty man was not filled with pique,
'You people wear plus-fours
Mine are minus fours',
He said, tongue firmly wedged in his cheek.

For tea with the royal couple he got an invitation
To the Palace he went, representing his nation.
This man of thrift
Intrigued Queen Mary and George fifth
And the commoner gaped in utter stupefaction.

What would he wear? England did watch.
He wore a shawl, a loyally dangling watch
Sandals, and loincloth, people were dumbfounded
Gandhi's faith in this dress well-founded
His weird dress, however, the visit did not botch!

At the little upstart's whim the royal lip curved
Giving him a reprimand he thought he deserved.
By his thoughtlessness peeved
At the boycott of the Prince of Wales grieved
But impeccable in his attire Gandhi was unnerved!

'Don't stir up trouble in my Empire', the King said
Gandhi did not lose his cool, but was silent instead.
The King sermonized
His wrath Gandhi disguised
And refused to argue, cautious his tread!

Some sniggered, some watched tight-lipped
And one ventured to ask in accents clipped
Whether he was wearing enough
Unperturbed by this question tough
'The King had enough on', Gandhi quipped.

Absolutely annoyed by this royal meeting
Gandhi was with unvented ire seething
By his haughty air irked
But he was later perked
When he met Chaplain in an amiable meeting.

David Lloyd George, Britain's war time Prime Minister
Invited this man, who was no minister
To his farm at Churt, Surrey
Where the servants were in a flurry
Bustling out to meet this guest of the Prime Minister.

Gandhi was keen to meet Chaplain the legend
When told that he came from London's East End.
Although not a movie fan
Gandhi agreed to meet the man
Who hailed from the poor section of London East End.

They hailed from a small community, said the playwright
GB Shaw to the man, who stood for the right.
He called himself 'Mahatma Minor'
And Gandhi 'Mahatma Major'.
Myriad topics they touched in ambience bright.

In England he stayed for days eighty four
Some found him a saint, some an eyesore
He won hearts through his humanity
His humor and accessibility
And made the loving children crave for more.

But alas, the minds he couldn't conquer
As they were still filled with rancour.
The policy of Divide and Rule
Was an ominous tool
Which intensified the ill-feeling and rancour.

For an honorable partnership he had pleaded
Maintaining that, in all dealings love was needed
But this simple eloquence
To them made no sense
And Gandhi's plea went unheeded!

Gandhi felt enmeshed in a dense fog
With his ideas few going the whole hog.
Equal partnership appeared elusive
British were unsupportive
With rampant bargaining, denser grew the fog.

To his way of thinking, they refused to bend
For Gandhi, this travail seemed to have no end.
But this figure
Of wealth meagre
Was a hit with the children of London's East End!

Gandhi with little children in England

On Uncle Gandhi, they heaped love in abundance
Intrigued by his homespun eloquence
In their love he basked
Countless questions they asked
His simplicity appealing to their innocence.

Of his visit, this was the redeeming feature
Despite his weird get up, a loved creature.
Relating stories of his childhood
He asked them to shun falsehood
And proved to be a well-loved teacher.

Although the conference was an utter failure
The Englishman was mesmerized by this soul pure.
Neither an impossible fanatic
Nor an idealist quixotic
This fact was brought home to them, for sure.

Gandhi and Ambedkar

MacDonald Award and the Poona Pact

On 17th August 1932, a communal award was announced
For depressed classes separate electorates it pronounced.
His worst nightmare confirmed
In humiliation utter Gandhi squirmed
Determined that this award had to be renounced.

Convinced that parochial loyalties would be created
And national unity would be debilitated
Triggering a dangerous trend
MacDonald proved to be no friend.
With Ambedkar he wanted things to be negotiated.

From the Hindu fold, they could not be separated.
The rift between them would be perpetuated
Was Gandhi's argument.
Nehru found his attitude truculent.
But the magic of his powers he had underestimated.

Soon the wave of opposition stronger grew.
He decided to go on a fast from 20th September 1932.
'Preposterous', the detractors said.
And the authorities saw red
But Gandhi was bent on a fast anew.

With this dubious award, he could not go along.
The policy of appeasement was inherently wrong.
Harmony in diversity was needed.
For Hindu-Harijan amity he pleaded.
With Ambedkar would follow negotiations long.

Losing Gandhi to the fast, was a possibility.
The country suffered the pain of anxiety.
To him it was a sublime penance
Which should be followed with reverence.
Preventing dismemberment of Indian society.

Ambedkar and his followers glumly surmised
It was a method of coercion, thinly disguised.
But Gandhi reiterated in outrage
That it would accentuate the cleavage
If none listened, he yearned to be sacrificed.

On 15th September, in a statement widely circulated
Banish untouchability, or sacrifice me, he stated.
Gandhi must not die
Amid many a sigh
Said the caste Hindu who now himself berated.

In no time, in Delhi Hindus, Harijans fraternised.
Streets, temples harmoniously hummed undisguised.
On Gandhi were eyes centered
As temples were freely entered
At this news Gandhi felt slightly energised.

Under the impact of his revolutionary fast
There were remarkable changes fast
Many temples stopped temple discrimination
Filling Gandhi with elation
None could be banned entry on the basis of caste.

Some temple priests scornfully their lips curved
At the treatment they were receiving undeserved.
Hindu students showed they cared
When they magnanimously shared
Seats which for the untouchables were reserved.

The sands of times were running out fast.
In determined lines his face was cast.
The government was tense
Wanting to shift him to a private residence.
But it was in the jail that he wanted to fast.

At 12 am on 20th September began the fast
Lemon juice and honey were his meal last.
With immense faith imbued
By saying no to food
He had definitely created a blast.

Under the canopy of a tree on a cot he lay.
In his mind many thoughts did stray.
In the prison yard quiet
He braced himself for another fight
All his hidden resources in full play.

Under the mango tree in the jail
With him were Mahadev Desai and Patel.
These men two
Were joined by Sarojini Naidu
From Sabarmati Ashram came Ba looking frail.

The Hindu leaders met in Birla House in Bombay.
Solanki and Ambedkar were also in the fray.
Ambedkar, the lawyer eminent
In the atmosphere turbulent
From the chosen path, did not stray.

Meetings followed, negotiations reached a deadlock
Ambedkar, a bargainer hard, was like a rock.
No formula could be hammered out
The negotiators plagued by many a doubt.
Would Gandhi be able to endure this shock?

They could be empowered, if from Hindus separated.
Attitude of caste Hindus, Ambedkar always hated.
But it was Gandhi's dream
To let them remain in the mainstream
And therein a harmonious unity celebrated.

On 22nd, Ambedkar came to Gandhi's bed
Fear in his heart, caution in his tread.
I want my compensation,
He said in apprehension
Expecting a snub, but things had come to a head.

Of the prison, Sarojini became the doorkeeper.
In the shadows waited Death, the Reaper.
Gandhi was in pain intense
Everyone was tense
While the talks slipped into an impasse deeper.

Although to Ambedkar, it smacked of blackmail
He realised Gandhi was getting frail.
To everyone's pleasant surprise
He agreed to a compromise
Suddenly festive was the atmosphere in the jail.

That Ambedkar had agreed was a matter great.
Seats reserved for them were one forty-eight
In the legislature, as opposed to seventy one
After hectic bargaining a victory was won
This indeed carried a heavy weight.

From Calcutta Tagore came to sit by his friend ill.
'Floating on the tide of good news', Gandhi was still.
That late morn
He was withdrawn
But willingly yielded to Sarojini's will.

His blood pressure was alarmingly high
Death appeared to be nigh
The Poona Pact
Had required a lot of tact
But it was now time to heave a relieved sigh.

Two hundred people in the courtyard congregated.
Gandhi would break his fast, they were elated.
With anxiety gripped
They watched as orange juice he sipped
Breaking into smiles, though belated.

Come with a meaningful shower,
Tagore sang this hymn under the mango bower.
On that day sultry and hot
Soothing the people a lot
Infusing some joy in the one under the bower.

He now plunged into the torrent turbulent
Still sick in body, but in spirit buoyant.
One more bastion had to be won
Without the use of a gun
His heart throbbed in a wild tumult.

In the deep thickets of his inner wilderness
And in the nocturnal stillness
Many a dream rustled
With many hidden demons he wrestled
But he addressed himself to his new business.

The 21-Day Fast

8-28th May

A week long happy delirium followed
While the British government its ire swallowed
Gandhi was no longer in pain
India could now breathe again
Unprepared was the government for what followed.

The nation heaved a collective sigh
Was the end of untouchability nigh?
Gandhi was right
This curse couldn't go overnight
But for this cause, he was ready to die.

In the darkness, the crusader had kindled a flame.
Things would no longer be the same
To the sky it leapt
With a reformative zeal, the country it swept.
Soon into a raging fire turned this tiny flame.

Gandhi with Sarojini Naidu

The crusade started in right earnest.
The lone crusader put himself to another test.
He started a campaign great
Never resting, being his trait.
To this task he wanted to give his best.

He started *Harijan*, a weekly new
Which, with his rapier touch he did imbue.
This was another gain
In the promotion of the campaign
But for the Sanatanists an unpalatable brew.

He realised untouchability was a sin vast.
Over his brow a cloud had been cast.
Its horrifying magnitude
Needed a change in attitude.
As a penance, he yearned for another fast.

Gandhi was a prisoner, still not free
Started fasting on 8th May, nineteen thirty-three.
While the father of the nation
Yearned for self-purification
Apprehensive of his death, Britain set him free.

But for the weak Gandhi, this was no big deal
With equanimity, he went through this ordeal
At Lady Thackersey's house Parnakuti
He carried out his solemn duty
Hidden in his fragile body a strong will.

Accompanied by Desai, Sarojini and Patel
To the mansion was driven the man frail.
Filled with frustration
He hated ostentation
Mirabehn implored from Sabarmati jail.

This hilltop mansion which housed this celebrity
Was magnificently equipped, servants aplenty.
Gandhi was calm
The doctors in alarm
Worried about the man aged four and sixty!

Not to go on fast, by friends cajoled.
Of the risks by the doctors, he was told.
Like a skeleton he looked
On the fast hooked
Oblivious to what said the young and the old!

To and fro from the mansion the doctors walked.
At this attention unnecessary, Gandhi baulked.
Kasturba sat by his side
Valiantly Death was defied
At the doctors, thus a snook he cocked!

On 29th May, with orange juice, he broke his fast.
Miraculously for twenty-one days he did last.
Armed with moral tenacity
And a rare equanimity
Now he was on the road to recovery fast.

He drank milk on the doctor's insistence
Sitting up on bed with or without assistance.
As his health returned
Anew his mind churned
With his sincerity and inherent resilience.

On his release he had suspended civil disobedience.
About his next move the government was tense.
With a mind calm
He sent a telegram
To Willingdon, but the Viceroy refused to see sense.

The possibilities of peace, he wanted to explore.
He was snubbed by Willingdon who was sore.
Refused an interview
Which he did rue
On 1 August he was again outside the prison door!

Now started a cat-and-mouse game undignified
Soon he was released, but within Poona confined.
Was his patience being tested?
He was soon rearrested
As the restraint order he had willfully defied!

The Government seethed with resentment
He was sentenced to a year's imprisonment
On 16 August, he went on fast
Was this another blast?
And for the authorities a grave predicament!

To the government's indignation intense
He wanted to work for untouchables without hindrance.
The government aghast
At another fast
utterly confused, nothing seemed to make any sense.

On 20th August, government was worried how to save
The frail prisoner who so incredibly brave
In his condition
A rapid deterioration
He was shifted to Sasoon hospital, in condition grave.

Now, unlike the earlier fasts, water he refused.
At this preparation for Death, all were confused.
His body's reaction
To willful starvation
Was painfully alarming, none was amused!

His eyes were deep sunken, he looked ill.
No longer keen to exert his strong will.
The government felt
Death lurked in stealth
How to tackle this man who was a prisoner still?

Eventually, over this dilemma they tided.
And to release their sick prisoner they decided
So the shriveled up bird
On August twenty third
Was released and to Thackersey mansion guided!

On a stretcher he was carried, looking gray
'Will yourself to live', said Andrews insisting he obey.
To this man of grit
Nehru paid a visit
With him Gandhi discussed where his duty lay!

Now he suspended civil disobedience.
Filling the intelligentsia with resentment intense
His colleagues despaired
Were his mental powers impaired?
To them this suspension smacked of nonsense.

To Nehru, this came as a stab of pain
For Bose the decision was not sane.
Gandhi had failed
Many openly wailed
That their sacrifices had been in vain.

Sabarmati Ashram was home for eighteen years
As an act of penance, without shedding tears.
This man of dignity
Abandoned this ashram at Sabarmati
Although this act his heart did pierce.

In central provinces, Wardha was a town small
Here in a little ashram lived a man tall.
Vinobha Bhave his name
His claim to fame
Was that, nonviolence was also his call!

Now for a period of nine months this sage
From Wardha set out on a pilgrimage.
Where he had shifted
After having gifted
His ashram which for some was an outrage.

His pilgrimage aimed at removal of untouchability.
Which for him was a millennial monstrosity.
On days cloudy and sunny
Untiringly, he collected money
Making people wonder at his tenacity!

It was a unique movement, never before seen.
People flocking to meet this man lean.
In gestures magnanimous
Women surrendered ornaments precious
To make still more sacrifices they appeared keen.

But lo and behold, the movement came to a halt.
Was someone guilty of a gross fault?
Hindus with black flags armed
Around the crusader swarmed
Why had they brought the movement to a halt?

By the orthodox Hindus jeered and taunted.
He now walked to the next village undaunted.
To his utter gall
They formed a human wall
Around his hut, black flags they flaunted.

Untouchability is doomed, Gandhi claimed.
But the orthodox Hindus were still enflamed.
Vicious questions they posed
His movement opposed
Gandhi wondered whether they would ever be tamed.

Northern Bihar had to drink a bitter brew
In January 1934, when an earthquake of sinister hue.
Towns were reduced to rubble
It was grave trouble
Gandhi now decided to tackle this calamity new!

The news, filled him with consternation
On March 1934, in the tour there was interruption
This monster he would definitely slay
But now he knew where his duty lay
On this count, there was no confusion.

Over broken roads to Motihari, the traveller travelled
The victims with myriad problems bedevilled.
Some looked askance
Some comforted by his presence
The orthodox Hindus still at him barbs leveled.

They jeered, standing on both sides of the road
Halting his tour he could ill afford
At Jassidi in south Bihar
They attacked his car
Undaunted he walked on, carrying his moral sword.

From village to village marched the party small
Attending to the victims at their leader's call.
This man with lanky grace
Of fatigue showed no trace
Onward walked he with his party small.

From shacks people ran to meet the man slight.
Under a villager's roof spending many a night.
Many could be seen
Offering him coconut green
Despite their impoverished plight.

Lanterns in hands there were nocturnal visitors.
Under a tree they discussed the millennial curse.
Put away the sin of untouchability
Gandhi said with tenacity
To his cause the opposition was getting worse.

In June 1934, an attempt was made on his life
When in a car in Poona with his wife.
Though unharmed, it was dastardly
And also cowardly
But pierced his heart as though with a knife.

Now, another cloud on the horizon was cast
In a meeting in Ajmer, a Hindu high caste
Was on the head struck
Gandhi was dumb-struck.
Upon himself he took the blame, vowing a fast.

Six lakh rupees for *Harijan* fund he did raise
In July 1934, in Wardha, fasting for seven days
With problems bedeviled
12,500 miles he travelled
At age sixty five, a glow on his face.

Sevagram where he had built his cottage
Became the hub of political pilgrimage
His advice was sought
Which meant a lot
In the villagers trying to infuse moral courage.

He talked of the nutritional value of food
Emphasising self-reliance which was good.
For the villager poor
Gandhi was an untiring doer
With resilience on myriad issues he did brood.

In October 1934, he had resigned from the party
It could ill-afford to ignore this man of integrity.
On rural economics
His mind he did fix
With determination fierce, attending to the nitty-gritty.

His resignation was not an angry reaction
For himself he was seeking freedom of action.
He didn't see eye-to-eye
So with a sad sigh
With the Congress he decided to have no interaction.

In his mental powers there was no diminution
Working for village industries following his intuition.
Honing his nonviolent strategy
Staunchly adhering to veracity
Sincerely paving the way for a new revolution.

Replace the brush with the village-made broom
For the use of indigenous kikar there was room.
In his new quest
This was his request
If 'Swadeshi' was not revived, there would be doom.

Out of their slumber the villagers he tried to awake
This was absolutely necessary for their sake.
Rural India's transformation
Was now his determination
Convinced that mills brought unemployment in their wake.

Work in the village was the work of a plodder
But in his mission, the man did not dodder
Whether this activity
Had the capability
Of helping India, this was mental fodder.

Emphasis on primitive economy would perpetuate poverty
And the main goal would surely be a casualty.
This was the apprehension
But to this new passion
Gandhi clung on, with his overpowering veracity.

A self-contained village was his cherished dream
To his detractors utopian it did seem
But this man practical
Ignored the remarks critical
And surged forward, in the pursuit of this dream.

Nonviolence cannot stand on a factory civilisation.
To build self-contained villages was his reiteration.
The government was restive
Was this some new offensive
A plan astute by a wily politician?

Gandhi tours India to generate support for Satyagraha

Congress in Office

In 1935, the parliament enacted a constitution new
Which, was of course, long overdue
It was a vehicle in low gear
Was India's fear
The budget outside the federal legislature's purview.

The Viceroy and the governor had overriding powers
The granting of self-government only a farce
Resentment was all pervasive
At this constitution unimpressive
Faith in this constitution was naturally sparse.

India was unripe for democracy, the British assumed
A charter of slavery! Nehru fumed
The government was tight lipped
Congress by a dilemma gripped
They would still be powerless, it presumed.

Though it offered responsibility without power
Constructive work was the need of the hour
This was Gandhi's view
And he fully knew
In that direction, they needed to go far.

Even within the framework of the new constitution
Constructive work would be carried out, the intention
Unemployment and poverty
Could be tackled with probity
This thought brought the much-needed consolation.

So, after a lot of reflection
The Congress decided to contest the election
Although aggrieved
It strongly believed
Anti-national elements would win the election.

In February 1937, results of the elections were declared
In provincial legislatures, it had not badly fared.
In UP, Orissa, CP, Madras, Bihar
The Congress had gone far
Winning clear majorities, the government it had dared.

It was the largest party in the NWFP and Assam
For the government, this was cause for alarm
Half the seats it won in Bombay
This was no child's play
And many an Indian heart this did warm.

To be or not to be was now the question
In the Congress manifesto no clear mention
What was to be done
If majorities it won
In the provincial legislatures, now there was tension.

Ministry formation some vehemently opposed
And myriad queries they posed
Some filled with verve
Thought masses it could serve
Governor's powers be curtailed, others interposed.

Gandhi tried to harmonise the opposing views
Criticism was sharp, assuming various hues
Filled with indignation
At this unjust situation
Through mediation the tension he tried to defuse.

Pursued the socio-economic agenda of the Congress
The peasants half-starved, rampant the mess.
Set an example of frugality
Try to alleviate poverty
Thus he exhorted the ministers of the Congress.

The two planks were prohibition and education
He wanted these to be followed with determination.
Not to overrate academic instruction
Was his exhortation
Character-building and skills to be given recognition.

His plan included in Wardha scheme of education
Led to joy and an intense mental stimulation.
But critics were not few
Who did strongly rue
Teachers would be slave-drivers their speculation.

Along novel lines, the educationists started to think
In unreceptive minds, the scheme started to sink
Substitute bookish learning
By coordinated training
They seemed to have found the missing link.

India had to flourish in her own climate
She cannot grow on foreign victuals he did state.
The curriculum modified
He felt edified
This reorientation of education, an impetus great.

The English language had literary treasures ample
But Hindi it couldn't be allowed to trample.
Let's build on our own heritage
Hindi is our own language
Not unlike English, it also has treasures ample.

The ministries attempted improvement in education
Mother tongue became the medium of instruction
With a sense of elation
Also some tension
He hoped this would improve the deplorable situation.

Rural indebtedness was a problem grave
The ministries tackled this with a resolve brave
With Gandhi as their guide
Many innovations were tried
For agrarian legislation the path they did pave.

To his utter dismay, he realised
That corruption in Congress was ill-disguised.
Violence and untruth reigned
By this he was pained
Motivating them to follow Truth, which he prized!

For crumbs of office there was scramble mad
At this, Gandhi's heart was unbearably sad.
This was an unhealthy trend
Its ways Congress should mend
Frittering away its energy in rivalries was bad.

Form peace brigades, exhorted Gandhi, distraught.
The communal animosity was with dangers fraught.
Indiscipline and fanaticism
And rampant communalism
Had all his ideals come to naught?

He was bowed down by disillusionment great.
There was mutual suspicion, rancor and hate.
It was not the time
Nor the clime
To form peace brigades was a responsibility great.

Gandhi leading Quit India protest

Cripps Mission

In 1939 on his first visit came Cripps tall
To an ailing Gandhi, he promptly paid a call.
On the floor of his hut he lay ill
But his sense of humor intact still
He was polite, but for Cripps the situation droll.

With a lopsided smile on his lips
Gandhi offered a stool to Stafford Cripps
In sardonic tones
As a concession to English bones
While a smile continued to hover on his lips.

On 27th March 1942, he went to 3, Victoria Road
To discuss with Cripps a plan which thought was bold.
Two lawyers were face to face
But Gandhi found the plan a disgrace
Take the next plane home, Cripps he told.

Gripped with misgivings, for him it was not straight.
India would never fall for the bait.
He wanted India undivided
Muslim League this idea derided
And vigourously campaigned for a Pakistan separate.

To India's intense pain and discomfiture
Somewhere in the vague, distant future
India was set to become
A dominion in the United Kingdom
This ambiguity filled Gandhi with intense displeasure.

For full control over defense India craved
Without that control it would still be enslaved
Hope undernourished
Alas, soon perished
It perked up, as many storms it had braved.

National Herald called it a stage-managed show
Uniformly rejected, its procedure was slow
And a stunning shock
That even a friend could mock
The Congress sentiments and could not offer more.

This disconcerting news, didn't impress them a bit.
At the Cripps fiasco their brows they knit
The Congress was dissatisfied
Its hopes had been belied
Upon the idea of a novel agitation, it hit.

Quit India Movement

For Britain, were the sands running out?
They were in dire straits, there was no doubt.
Such a viewpoint though painful
Gandhi's influence was baneful
They were buckling under this resistance stout.

India was declared 'a party to war' by Linlithgow
To her self-respect this was a great blow.
War ordinances were promulgated
On Indian nerves this grated
Now Congress got ready to tackle its foe.

Followed a strong wave of frustration.
From bad to worse became the situation.
At Japan's imminent offensive
India grew restive.
What could be done to stem this tide of desperation?

Quit India Movement

Vociferously Jinnah demanded a Muslim state.
Was there no way to come out of this stalemate?
Distraught did Gandhi grow
After the Cripps fiasco.
The all-pervasive cynicism he really did hate.

Unbearable had become the rampant humiliation,
So one fine morning he came to a decision.
He deemed fit
That Britain should quit
As its reign had given rise to suffocation.

On 7th August 1942, came the Quit India Resolution,
It was finally time for India's emancipation.
The action plan nebulous
But the man tenacious
Put forth this demand with a new determination.

Entrust India to God or to a situation anarchic
Nonviolence would arise out of that situation chaotic.
He ardently did feel,
To make a final appeal,
To the Viceroy before taking any step drastic.

Their demand now was complete independence
Which they hoped to achieve without violence
The yearning for freedom grew
And on 8th August, 1942
Gandhi exhorted his countrymen to follow nonviolence.

Next morning the Congress leaders were arrested
Enough had the authorities' endurance been tested
With no weapon in their armoury,
Armed with a zeal revolutionary
The commoner was awake, enough he had rested.

Nonviolent non-cooperation was no mere platitude,
The alien government had reduced them to servitude.
On a moral high,
They had to do or die.
Freedom would then be a certitude.

Robbed of leadership they now faced a severe test
Still they surged forward, fired by a moral zest.
Swept by a turbulent gale
There were arrests wholesale.
Indians were killed but there was no inquest.

Out of their slumber people had been jerked.
They had straightened their spines, felt perked.
Now thoroughly vitalised
British ire ill-disguised
Spluttered wondering where the danger lurked.

The rising and simmering discontent,
Was churned up into a wrathful ferment,
Filled with gall
In places all
People openly seethed with resentment.

For the government things were a mess,
It followed a policy of suppression ruthless.
Newspapers were throttled,
But emotions long bottled,
Burst forth in a patriotic zest breathless.

It brought forth a transformation complete
With unprecedented zeal, the air replete
Students—girls and boys
Shunning all joys
Were up in arms in an incredible feat.

In trying to crush this upsurge of spirit
The desperate authorities did not wince a bit.
They were extremely peeved
The masses swayed and heaved.
Leaderless they marched on, with moral grit.

This superior movement had an all-embracing quality
Investing every one with a rare spontaneity.
This weapon of self-expression
Shunned territorial aggression
Filling the high and mighty with perplexity.

Gandhi with Mahadev Desai

Mahadev Desai

1 January 1892-15 August 1942

In the Aga Khan palace he was interned
Outside there was a reign of terror he learned
He felt checkmated
And utterly frustrated
That his offer to plead with the Viceroy had been spurned.

Less than a week after his internment
Gandhi suffered a colossal bereavement
Mahadev Desai suddenly died
His anguish Gandhi couldn't hide
Unable to come to terms with this tragic moment.

At this juncture nothing could be worse
He lost Mahadev in circumstances adverse
His untiring industry
And warm personality
Had endeared him to Gandhi for twenty-five years.

Desai was twenty-five and Gandhi forty-eight
When he joined the man great
Born in poverty
Loyalty marked his personality,
Which Gandhi had judged with an instinct accurate.

On 4 September 1915, two friends walked
Along the Sabarmati River, they hardly talked
These friends two
Contemplative grew
Stopping at Ellis Bridge where cattle flocked.

To join the 46-year-old lawyer he had decided
To Narhari Parikh, this yearning he confided
The youth 23-year-old
Had taken a decision bold
On this day by Gandhi to be guided.

The more he met him the more his resolve grew
Yearning to join this man true.
A vague aspiration
Soon becoming a vibrant intention
Of following his heart, this he knew.

Gandhi wanted Mahadev to stay with him
This was not a mere fad or whim
The man inspired confidence
And Gandhi could sense
That he could prove a boon to him.

This clarion call, Mahadev couldn't resist
Destiny had planned this historic tryst
So on 3rd November, nineteen seventeen
This man sharp and keen
Went to Godhra, the opportunity not to be missed.

Gandhi was attending the first Gujarat conference.
To Champaran, he was to go after this conference.
By Gandhi enjoined
His entourage he joined
Which went to Bihar after this conference.

For twenty-five years lasted this relationship
Undergoing many a hurdle and hardship
Now Mahadev was dead
His heart bled
At the cruel snapping of this unique friendship!

All this unspooled in Gandhi's mind
As he tried to endure this blow unkind
His remarkable humility
And selfless fidelity
Were indeed rare and difficult to find.

On the earth he had been only fifty years
Gandhi felt as though under a curse
In this man's excellence
He had reposed confidence
Now he was gripped by a sadness fierce.

Without the least trace of ego
He had reduced himself to a zero
Privy to his anguish
And many a heartfelt wish
Often pandering to the whims of his hero!

While his guru in troubled waters fished
Many difficult tasks he had accomplished.
With ardour unflappable
He was indispensable
To Gandhi, who on him his affection lavished.

Living with him was not an easy task
But still in his glory he loved to bask.
This man unique
Lucre did not seek
In serving him his happy feelings he couldn't mask!

With Gandhi his personality he had merged
Doing whatever his guru urged.
Always by his side
Matching stride with stride
When on the scene people converged.

A leading figure in his own right
He stayed away from political limelight
To a higher cause subjugated
A niche for himself he created
By translating Gandhi's biography with a rare insight.

On 15 August 1942, Death waited to render a knock.
He failed to get up for the Prayer at 4 o'clock.
This was something rare
But he did get up after the prayer
Now all indulged in banter and cheerful talk.

Sushila Nayyar massaged Gandhi, happy her mind.
Relentless Death waited to render a blow unkind.
It was cruelly bent
With a glee triumphant
To yank them away from this happy frame of mind.

There were sounds of laughter from Sarojini's room
Oblivious to the stealthily lurking doom
With face flushed
Sushila Nayyar rushed
When someone called from Sarojini's room!

She checked his pulse as she sobbed
Mahadev Desai's heart no longer throbbed.
In panic, their hands they kneaded
In its mission Death had succeeded
Of a wonderful friend they had been robbed.

A few moments back all were in cheerful mood
Now they stood dumbfounded by this shock rude.
Crushed was the laughter
Gandhi came soon after
Confronted by the tragedy, unblinking he stood!

His favorite son and secretary was no more
Gandhi's heart had been pierced to the core.
Feeling dismembered
Sadly he remembered
The day when a young man had come to his door.

Of his Guru's experiments, the harbinger
This writer, philosopher was also a poet, a singer.
His Guru was a celebrity
He considered himself a non-entity
At his temperament, none could raise a finger.

With Gandhi he totally identified
Managing his time, seeing that it was properly utilised
The iron code of ashram life
Was adhered to by him and his wife
To Gandhi now he was inextricably tied!

With a sigh of weary resignation
He accepted this untimely separation
Nothing could now be done
Though a father had lost his son
Alas, the sun had set with no indication!

The government no longer callous
Showed no ill will or malice
The man great
They did cremate
In the open ground of Aga Khan Palace.

Kasturba's Death
22 February 1944

A shadow fell on the Aga Khan palace
Ah, life could be cruel and callous!
Death knocked at its door
On 22nd February 1944
When Kasturba fell victim to Death's malice.

Chronic bronchitis had taken her life
How sorely he missed his wife.
This woman remarkable
To Gandhi was indispensable
Pain pierced his body like a sharp knife.

His idiosyncrasies, she had borne all
Many a time filled with utter gall
The man diminutive
His grief accumulative
Sat huddled in a corner enveloped in a gloomy pall.

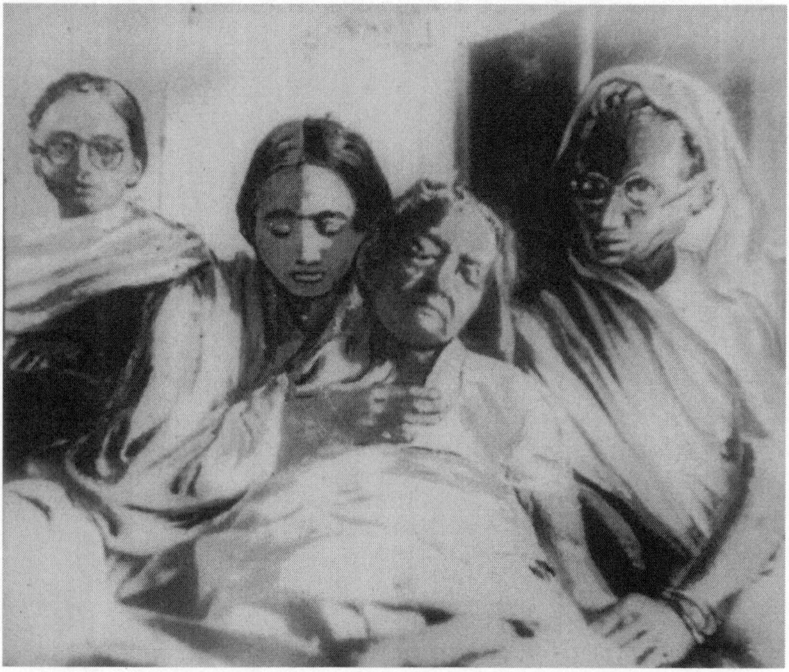

All her life she catered to her husband mighty.
This woman gentle, also full of piety.
At times, pliant
Sometimes defiant
But shackled by patriarchal society.

She had endured the authoritative streak in him
Stoically bearing many a fad and whim.
A husband caring
But often overbearing
Was now trying to valiantly face a situation grim.

Despite her husband's domineering personality
She still retained her individuality.
Tea and coffee she drank
From which Gandhi shrank
Often trying to browbeat him with wifely authority.

With her husband she had many a tiff
Well-conversant with his inclination to mischief.
Once in English broken
She had thus spoken
'I know my husband, he always mischief.'

Through the thick and thin of life
By his side had always been his wife.
In thunder and rain
In pleasure and pain
She had marched along through the rampant strife.

A woman gentle, with a keen sensibility
Not unaware of her husband's fallibility
To his eccentricities resigned
Performing the tasks assigned
Sometimes grudgingly, more often with sincerity.

With a painful mental shrug he accepted the inevitable.
But ah! His pain was so palpable
The hours leaden-footed
And sounds muted
Impassioned he sat, ruminating about life inscrutable!

His heart was heavy with despondence
Without her, tough the earthly existence.
The sweet fragrance
Of soothing incense
Wafted in, laden with chunks of remembrance.

A contented look suffused her face in his presence.
Many of her answers were laced with innocence.
Now, on this dark day
Before him lifeless she lay
Many a time, she had strained his patience.

Now the man patiently sat, shoulders stooped.
While memory upon memory stealthily trooped.
How the thirteen-year-old
Had entered his household
With unshed tears his eyes drooped.

By mutual bickering were their teens characterized
At times her irritation ill-disguised
Burst forth in a torrent
Which was, of course, never meant
To dent their bonds, though they mutually criticized.

She would be worried when he went on fast.
Now in his lap she had breathed her last.
Through the dramatic and mundane
The pleasure and the pain
She had been like a rock steadfast.

Gandhi with Jinnah

Cabinet Mission 1946

On 16th May 1946, the mission posed a compromise
A 3-tier constitution which they thought wise
Jinnah was obstinate
This mechanism delicate
With checks and balances he found unwise.

On the radio by the members the plan was explained.
In the debilitating heat, they felt drained.
In a mood mellow
Wavell quoted Longfellow
But, Jinnah petulantly complained.

In settling differences the mission failed.
The negotiators felt impotent, their plans had derailed.
Congress wanted an India united
By Jinnah this was derided
Its inprudent proposals he bewailed.

By the League, the mission was criticised.
Pakistan is the only solution, Jinnah emphasised.
Their plans were reduced to rubble
In the horizon loomed trouble.
Jinnah's wrath appeared undisguised.

Later, in Birla House, Mussorie, amid Pine trees
The lush greenery removed many a crease
By the Pine scent invigorated
On many issues they ruminated
In the cottage surrounded by the rejuvenating breeze.

On 8 June, to New Delhi in a car he returned
India's response to the Cabinet Mission burned
Congress had still not given its assent
Controversy reigned about the interim government.
With the horror of partition, his mind churned.

The demand for Pakistan Jinnah reiterated
It was the only course left open, he stated
In a mood dejected
The plan was rejected
Things had reached a stalemate.

For Jinnah it was not a moment of joy
When Nehru was invited by the Viceroy
He fumed while the sky turned grey
Fixing 16 August as Direct Action Day
Gandhi's peace call none willing to employ.

Direct Action Day
16 August 1946

No longer willing to deliberate
For a separate homeland, Jinnah was obstinate.
The cauldron started to bubble
Jinnah resolved to create trouble
No way was the impending doom going to mitigate.

He would destroy India, Jinnah thundered.
Houses were looted, shops plundered.
On this dark day
The sky was gray
Into an inferno the country had blundered.

Rapacious vultures on rooftops sat
The reigning slogan was tit for tat.
Inhumanity replaced humanity
Brutality was met with brutality
Many a dream on the street had fallen flat.

Gandhi in consultation with other Indian leaders just before independence

Lad key lengey Pakistan, up went the cry
People of myriad hues, the short and spry
With a rare zest filled
Many innocents killed
On retaliation bent and violence high.

Came the last Viceroy, Mountbatten, on the scene now
With leaders discussing the when, where and how
In a last bid to stem the rising flood
Of violence and senseless blood
Gandhi tried, none willing to listen to this peace dove.

Dismiss the Nehru government, he pleaded.
But they smelt a rat, his plea went unheeded
Partition was the only cure
Which he could not endure
His magic wand broken, the wizard no longer needed.

Now partition, tore the country apart
This completely broke Gandhi's heart
The leaders half elated, half confused
Also by a new spirit infused
Of a blood-stained dawn this was only the start.

On 14th August 1947, the communities two
In Calcutta celebrated freedom long overdue.
As though of hate purged
On the streets they converged
Dancing and singing with an ardour new.

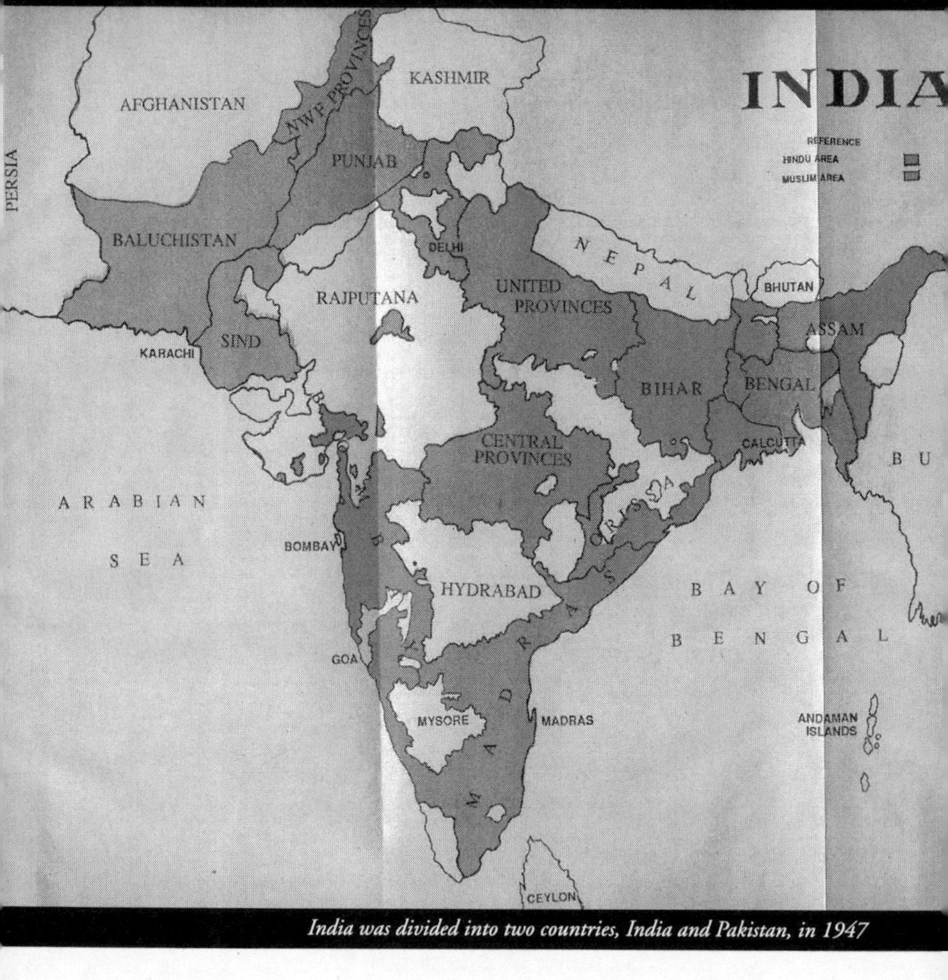

India was divided into two countries, India and Pakistan, in 1947

Migration

Gandhi was seized by intense restlessness
As lost humanity trudged towards homelessness.
The sick, in baskets they carried
Tired and absolutely harried
The police and military killed with thoughtlessness!

Some in bullock carts, and some on foot
Some fell to diseases and died en route.
Up above, the vultures did loom
While people headed toward doom
Down below, the human vultures continued to loot!

Over their shoulders the old they carried
Children and adults, the married and the unmarried.
Stumbling and tumbling
Fumbling and crumbling
Trudged on the uprooted humanity, utterly harried.

Mendacity abounded poisoning the air
Its toxic fumes polluted the atmosphere
At the butchery
And the savagery
The saintly warrior's heart was heavy with despair!

The country was in the throes of a holocaust
Alas, their homes and hearths the people had lost.
With regard scant
The old and the infant
Were also attacked—heavy the cost!

Facing mobs he preached love, compassion
Told the Armed Forces to shun corruption
His confidence was dented
On a scale unprecedented
People were being murdered in retaliation.

In the midst of frenzy, there were cases of chivalry
Which Gandhi felt was a good augury
One community helped another
Brother helped brother
The vanquished had won a victory.

Amidst the crossfire of hate and suspicion
Rampant bloodshed and chaotic confusion
Stood a figure
In clothes meager
Spreading love and banishing hate, tough his mission.

An eye-for-an-eye will make the whole world blind
Said this man veracious and kind
Mosques were damaged
Temples ravaged
For communal harmony and peace he pined.

Second October 1947 did not dawn like any day
Though it was the Mahatma's 78th birthday
He was restless
The fury relentless
Dampened his spirits, he could smell decay.

Demonic forces had unleashed orgies of hate
Love vanished as playmate fell upon playmate
People from small and big houses
Those with or without grouses
Upon each other pounced, the anguish great.

There was murder, mayhem and misery
Humans killing inhumanly in a show of grotesquery.
Heads were horrendously hacked
Homes ruthlessly ransacked
He felt like hanging his head at this savagery.

In a reprehensible chain of gore was India caught
Alas, all his efforts were coming to naught
There was misery and destruction
Abuse and retaliation
With grave portents was India fraught.

Mind-numbing violence was unleashed with impunity
As atrocity was heaped upon atrocity
For throats they swiftly lunged
Beheading some, in some daggers plunged
The air rife with venom and bellicosity.

In the rampant darkness, the lost one groped
For some succour they desperately hoped
Waiting for benediction
But there was only malediction
The free so called, were still shackled and roped.

How could one cling to one's sanity
When people indulged in cannibalistic ferocity?
Countless millions died
Some fell by the roadside
Incredible the actions of hate-ravaged humanity.

To stay in the sweepers' colony he could ill-afford
In this madness like a moral colossus, he strode
Under Nehru and Patel's insistence
The man who shunned munificence
Was driven to Birla House at 5, Albuquerque Road!

Refugees from the Punjab embittered and irate
Resided now in this colony in misery great
Unclaimed corpses like hopes forlorn
On the streets lay from dusk to dawn
Which overflowed with filth, and hate.

Humans were inhumanly butchered like sheep
Over this vile devastation Gandhi lost his sleep
His country burned
Gandhi's mind churned
He slipped into melancholy deep.

A Life magazine photo of the communal riots in India, and now Pakistan, in the last years of British rule.

At Hydari House
13 August-7 September 1947

In Calcutta the tables had been turned
With hidden fire, the Hindu hearts burned.
No longer was Suhrawardy the premier
But things had now become seamier
In young breasts, fratricidal strife churned.

For Direct Action Day, Hindus vengeance shrieked
With grim portents, the atmosphere creaked.
Blood was in the air
To soothe them none could dare
They recalled last year's streets blood-streaked.

On 9th August, Suhrawardy, in a mood chastened
With a mission to Gandhi's Ashram hastened.
He was strongly bent
On getting his assent
For dousing the flames, eyes on Gandhi fastened.

Afraid that the Hindus would erupt into retaliation
To pay off old scores, being their determination.
His dismay he couldn't hide
Calcutta needed to be pacified
This could be done only by Gandhi's cooperation.

From angry hearts violence had to be purged
Please stay back, Suhrawardy earnestly urged.
Through a mission joint
He tried to make a point
In young hearts, vitriol and venom surged.

Into the abandoned Hydari House moved the two
Beleaguered communities tirelessly to woo.
Faced by yet another rigour
The half-naked figure
Was now on another path of the fighter true!

The nation would soon witness juxtaposition
Of horrors and chimerical celebration.
Pomp and pageantry
And senseless savagery
Would appear hand in hand in a dubious celebration.

The soul of a suppressed nation at last found utterance
But alas, sad was the apostle of nonviolence.
The jubilant cheers
Were drowned in his fears
His skeletal face shorn of all exuberance.

In the communal dormitory of 151, Belighata Road
On a straw mat he lay, on his mind a heavy load.
Freedom at what cost
He felt utterly lost
Lamenting his coming to the end of the road.

Slowly he slipped into a sleep of sad exhaustion
Not for him the frenzy of joyous celebration
His dream had shattered
He felt bruised and battered
Devastated by his beloved country's laceration.

His anguish lay caged in his private island of pain.
Had all his efforts been merely in vain?
In the gloom of the dormitory
He mulled over this pyrrhic victory
At this dawn of freedom, joy he could not feign.

His hopes crashed, to the ground they clattered.
To the nation, Indian unity no longer mattered.
The gardener was tired
His tools mud-mired
The tapestry of the motherland lay tattered.

At 2 o'clock he got up with a heavy heart
Of the celebration he did not want to be a part.
The vicious turpitude
Of malevolent magnitude
Of an unending nightmare was only the start.

Violence now reached a mind-numbing crescendo
The peace messenger like an injured sparrow.
His garden over flowed with weeds
He had to attend to its needs
Alone—all alone he needed to hoe.

73-Hour Fast
1-4 September 1947

On 31st August, Gandhi had gone to bed
When from outside, he heard a stealthy tread
The voices grew shrill
On his mat he lay still
With lack of sleep his eyes were red.

Between sleep and wakefulness he lingered
In worry intense his forehead he fingered.
In anxiety he muttered
Heading towards the window shuttered
And then near the window he lingered.

Of darkened silhouettes there was confusion
In his mind, of memories old and new a fusion.
This way and that his neck he craned
Utterly devastated and overstrained
Wondering whether all this was a delusion.

Gandhi with the Mountbattens

In barged a mob and started kicking doors
In ire great, they were bent on using force.
Gandhi moved forward
He was no coward
Windows they smashed, their language coarse.

His palms he touched together in greeting
But, the mob in anger, was seething.
Someone threw a brick
Another swung a stick
None returned the Mahatma's greeting.

The Muslims inside should be surrendered
The irate Hindu mob in ominous tones thundered.
They had gone insane
Kill me, Gandhi cried in pain
Would they not see reason, he sadly wondered.

In the confusion, his voice got drowned
In wrath utter the angry mob frowned.
Danger did lurk
It had gone berserk
Vehemently opposed to any sane sound.

In the language of love well-versed
He shook his head as he was openly cursed.
Myriad thoughts churned in his brain
All his appeals were in vain.
With tear gas the enraged mob was dispersed.

The miracle of Calcutta was a nine-day wonder
The very next day, its peace was torn asunder
Not far from his residence
There was sickening violence
Gandhi wondered at this blunder!

With grief the half-naked figure was overwrought
The dire situation with lurking dangers fraught.
The man of nonviolence
Slipped into a sullen silence
Were all his efforts slowly coming to naught?

At two Muslim labourers grenades were thrown
Hearing which, he let out an audible moan.
To the site he rushed
Alas he was totally crushed
For the loss of sanity, he started to mourn.

This monumental problem had to be solved
To go on a fast unto death, he now resolved.
At the news of this fast
His disciples were aghast
Before his determination, their doubts dissolved.

On 1st September began Gandhi's penance
Could it stem this tide of violence?
As he lay on his fiery bed
Many a thought whirred in his head
Would this treatment bring them to repentance?

In his mind, despondence was set against tenacity
His heart bled at the loss of human sublimity
Streets were littered with the dead
The reigning colour was red
By darkness engulfed, he still pined for humanity.

The sounds of gunfire fell into his ears
It was the realisation of his worst fears
Would the fury never abate?
Why this rancor and hate?
He grew restless, eyes heavy with unshed tears.

On the streets of Calcutta there was a metamorphosis
On his bed, he lay, depleted his physical resources.
In happy smiles faces were wreathed
Lethal weapons were sheathed
Was it a requiem for the evil communal forces?

His strength started to drain quite fast
Delegations beseeched to call off the fast.
But Gandhi was adamant
Despite his cough persistent
His face in lines of determination cast.

The Muslims and Hindus walked arm-in-arm
In the streets these peace armies acted as balm.
Under the influence of the sage
The youth bottled up their outrage
Into the crowds, they stormed unmindful of the harm.

Down with hooliganism slogans, full stride
Vile villains rushed to his bedside and cried.
Suhrawardy was abused
Of atrocities accused
Not to lose his composure, he also tried.

A dramatic effect followed his fast
Through which he hoped to address a problem vast.
Ruffians no longer surly
Scoundrels villainous and burly
Pleaded with him to put an end to the three-day fast.

They would keep the peace they intoned
Never would they resort to violence they moaned
It was an incredible sight
A frail man, with immense moral might
Beseeched by muscular men, strong boned.

A carload of arms was surrendered
Saving a life, leaving peace unsundered.
They signed a pledge.
No longer the nation on edge
Of an abyss into which it had almost blundered.

On 4th September, he ended the fast
For seventy-three chaotic hours it did last
To the savage butchery
Was this a lull temporary?
Had mayhem really become a thing of the past?

Now there was a semblance of peace
But Gandhi was still filled with unease
The man so painfully small
Had mesmerized one and all
What if they revert to madness, his brows did crease.

Fragile hope had into hopelessness slipped
The façade of joyous freedom had been ripped
Gandhi was sad
At the scenario mad
Of its grandeur, a new nation had been stripped.

By communal riots Delhi was paralysed
Gandhi's horror could not be disguised.
Hearts filled with malice
People ruthless and callous
Was this the freedom, so preciously prized?

The shattering of hopes was now loud and clear
He shuddered as nimble-footed disaster drew near
The people misguided
He vehemently chided
In vain trying to wipe many a tear.

In the Purana Quila camps, welcomed by jeers
While soothing them his eyes glistened with tears.
Around his car the Muslim refugees whirled
Their lips in derision curled
Still, in a voice weak, he tried to quell their fears.

The atmosphere, of hostility reeked
The refugees in contemptuous tones shrieked
Mouths contorted with rage
Mocked the seventy-seven-year-old sage
Saddened, he watched, ignoring the bones that creaked.

'Death to Gandhi', in wrath they cried
Almost engulfed by this outraged human tide
The ground under him rocked
In a whisper to the mob, he talked
To restore sanity the frail man tried.

Embittered refugees expressed their ire unshackled
At his fraternal message they derisively cackled.
Amidst sad sighs
And tears in his eyes
He spoke of love while the people heckled.

Some were indignant some brazenly rude
But Gandhi with a spirit of love was imbued
Though on hostile terrain
Love and forgiveness his refrain
Ultimately, their frenzy, the little man subdued.

Anger burned in both Hindu and Muslim eyes
The Hindus maligned him as a Muslim in disguise.
With hearts sore
Vengeance they swore
Gandhi lost his sleep, troubled by their cries.

A Hindu Fifth Columnist, the Muslims said
At this vilification, his tired heart bled.
Devastated at the moral depravity
And the loss of tolerance and charity
The anguished man now wanted to be dead!

To wispy hope, he clung in uncertainty
In agony regarding this Hindu Muslim unity.
No longer could he tarry
And follow his itinerary
Calcutta was calm, elsewhere there was insanity.

Riot followed riot with sickening regularity
Violence unleashed with a chilling familiarity.
Helplessly they railed
But utterly failed
Would this malady continue in perpetuity?

Gandhi was always ready to negotiate with the enemy to ensure justice and peace.

Final Fast
13-18 January 1948

In the cabinet there was mutual suspicion
He could see no reason for jubilation
Filled with great ire
He felt he was on his funeral pyre
From this helplessness, he wanted liberation.

India was poised on the verge of destruction
Unanswered went his imploration
The apostle of nonviolence
Sought a glorious deliverance
Yearning for communal harmony and cohesion.

The Inter-religious killing filled him with dread
He could not rest, while his country bled.
Outraged was his moral sensibility
Often succumbing to irascibility
His heart wept at the rampant bloodshed.

A decision flashed across his mind at last
On 12th January he announced that he would fast.
He felt he was out of a maze
After brooding for three days
His depression now a thing of the past.

He could hardly wait for this fast
Which started on 13th and was his last
Although in poor health
Through this fast unto death
He wanted to cleanse all hearts of hate.

The loss of harmony he did mourn
For peoples' sins he wanted to atone
Through this fast self-purificatory
He wanted to fight the grotesquery
If none responded, he would walk alone!

The nights were chilly, the days cold
Give up the fast, by many he was told
With a resolve firm he began the fast.
After a meager repast
Into the garden he moved in the afternoon cold.

In the morn, Patel, Nehru, Azad he had received
For his poor health, they had grieved
They were filled with fear
But Gandhi was in good cheer
And at their concern, absolutely peeved.

There were Muslim, Parsi and Buddhist prayers
Sushila Nayyar was plagued by myriad fears
With a strong determination
And faith in profusion
Ahead he forged, wiping humanity's tears.

To the prayer he walked with a determined gait
From every heart, resolved to banish hate
The man with no guile
Faced the congregation with a smile
With his weapon, hatred hoping to eradicate.

The balances owed to Pakistan, a heavy weight
On this issue he always talked straight
Although it had supporters few
It was Gandhi's view
India's duty to pay the amount could not wait.

14th January was another chilly dawn
Late in the morning, a meeting was held in the lawn
Gandhi was physically weak
But justice he did seek
On this bone-chilling morn.

Five hundred and fifty million rupees was under discussion
To be paid to Pakistan as a moral obligation
Gandhi and Nehru insisted
While Patel protested
No solution could be found to this bone of contention.

Peace and harmony had been ripped apart
Of an uneasy period, this was just the start
Violence was at its peak
He yearned to speak
The massacres in Karachi and Punjab bled his heart.

In the afternoon, to the prayer meeting he walked
Of his vision of a new holy Pakistan he talked.
There was rampant butchery
And widespread savagery
With rancor his beloved country rocked!

The same day there was an unsavory occurrence
Sikhs from the West Punjab screamed vengeance.
Storming towards Birla House spitting fire
Nehru was filled with ire
Dumbstruck by their verbal violence!

'Death to Gandhi', shouted the Sikhs irate
From his car Nehru dashed to them straight
At this ominous utterance
About the apostle of nonviolence
He was fuming with a rage great.

'Kill me first', he rejoined in agitation.
His entire body shaking with indignation
At this verbal assault
The Sikhs realised their fault
And scurried away in utter humiliation!

The third day a letter arrived from Patel
To Gandhi, an additional burden was this mail.
Patel had resigned
Doubts assailed Gandhi's mind
In a severe imbroglio was the man frail!

After sending the letter, Patel to Kathiawar flew
Meetings were addressed by Jawaharlal Nehru.
To Birla House people converged
For communal amity Prasad urged
The deterioration in Gandhi's condition grew!

Demonstrations favoured Hindu-Muslim unity
These sane voices mitigated his anxiety.
With pure pleasure his face lit
When the Mountbattens paid him a visit
For making a rapier thrust, this was an opportunity.

'It takes a fast to bring you', retorted the man witty.
Despite his debility, of humor he had no paucity.
With a rapier wit he was gifted
In embarrassment, they shifted
Amused by the frail man's mental agility.

Photo by Bradley Smith

Mahatma Gandhi with Louis Fischer and Rajkumari Amrit Kaur

Fight for Right

From his hot bath, he dictated with care.
Rs 55 crore was Pakistan's share
The amount India should pay
Without any delay, he did say
Pyarelal lifted him to put him in a chair!

It was the third day, and Gandhi was weak
But for the Muslims, justice he did seek
He had lost weight
With effect immediate
The government heeded the advice, the scenario bleak!

In the porch of Birla House he lay on a cot.
His well-wishers were a worried lot.
His crouched position
Caused great tension
With grave danger was his condition fraught.

An unending queue of well-wishers filed past
Worried that his condition was deteriorating fast.
Speaking through a microphone from his cot
He asked people to stem the rot
Prayers were hummed by people of every caste.

On the fourth day, Gandhi was in pain
Azad begged him to take citrus juice in vain.
Death he did not dread
Cautious was the doctor's tread
Would he survive the fast, their worry main.

He desperately hoped for the return of sanity
Wishing harmony to replace enmity.
His guide was God, the infallible
With spirit indomitable
He was prepared to face any eventuality.

On the fifth day, he received copious mail
But alas he continued to be frail
People of every community
Were reduced to pity
That he was getting progressively frail.

Frantically, Prasad worked behind the scene
For an acceptable solution he was keen.
Gandhi was serious
At times delirious
Misgivings churned in his mind, unseen.

His well-wishers were at the end of their tether
But on 18th January Gandhi was better
The situation was full of gravity
Committees aware of their responsibility
Under Prasad attended to an important matter.

For an end to the strife, Gandhi pined
On the morning of the 18th, a pledge was signed.
Hundred delegates from Prasad's house
And Nehru and Azad rushed to Birla House
Their faces with worry lined.

All differences were for the time being eradicated
The leaders of major communities persuaded
To promise the safety
Of the Muslim honor and property
Gandhi no longer felt emaciated.

His physical presence, the country needed
Discontinue the fast, the leaders pleaded
The assemblage waited
With breath bated
Wondering whether their plea would be heeded.

Would he or would he not, was the question
Giving rise to a rampant apprehension.
On him were fixed all eyes
Their fears they could ill-disguise
Seconds ticked, minutes passed, deep his introspection.

Many a detractor his teeth grated
Some poured scorn some were irritated.
This sublime penance
To some was sheer nonsense
Some by this great symbol morally elevated.

Weighing the pros and cons of a decision long-awaited
Gandhi was sunk in reflection, people waited.
Deep in thought
Sat he on a cot
Many an irksome point, he silently debated.

Did they really mean what they said?
Or were they doing it out of dread?
Tension heightened
People were frightened
But slowly things came to a head!

When he said he would break the fast.
Followed sighs that he had agreed at last.
With parched lips
He took a few sips
Of orange juice, and thus broke the fast!

He could live for 125 years, he quipped
While slowly from the glass, he sipped.
Outside, the rain pitter-pattered
Now, nothing else mattered
The communal evil, in the bud was nipped!

But alas this was too premature a thought
There was still all-pervasive rot.
Some minds were still deranged
Alas, hearts had not changed
With grim portents, the climate was fraught.

The six-day fast had brought people to sanity
Giving the Muslims a sense of security.
The noble son
Had a battle won
Succeeding in relieving the rampant anxiety.

The concession to the Muslims many found undue
Their impatience and frustration grew.
They would wreck vengeance
On the soldier of nonviolence
This was the mindset of a misguided few.

They could not touch his moral height
So found this concession not right.
The demon of barbarism
Stole a march over humanism
Setting a brazen example of physical might!

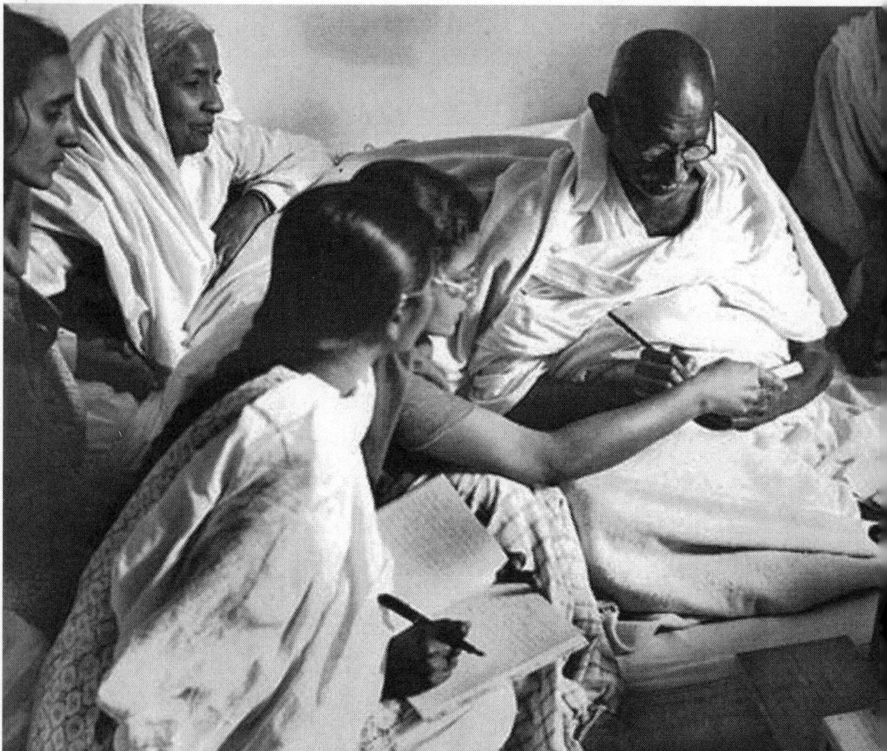

Gandhi with young disciples

Loved and Hated

The victim was being ruthlessly stalked
His ideals were being brazenly mocked.
On twentieth January
Another grotesquery
Was committed, the nation was shocked!

The security police was utterly irked
In the shadows, the demon lurked.
Hatred was still in the air
But this man rare
Shunned armed protection, feeling perked.

Armed with a guncotton slab and a grenade
A man surged forward, unafraid
He was on a mission of hate
In the shadows, Death was in wait.
Onward came the people, unaware of the plan laid!

On that day, he faced the congregation
Oblivious to the diabolical machination.
Sitting on a raised platform
As was the norm
He talked, people listened in fascination.

For a glimpse they came from every nook
Craning their necks for a better look.
Some neatly attired
Some shabby and tired
Suddenly with an explosion the earth shook!

Was it some soldier practicing sham fighting?
The tension was indeed nail-biting
Manubehn was absolutely terrified
What if Gandhi had died?
A man was seen, furtively a fuse lighting!

By a peasant woman in Gandhi's vicinity.
In no time, he was interrogated with alacrity.
He did mention
His intention
Killing the apostle of nonviolence. What insanity.

In a conspiracy, was he the chief conspirator?
What had turned him into a Gandhi hater?
In horror the country gaped
He had narrowly escaped
Questions buzzed around regarding this traitor!

Madan Lal Pahwa was the man's name
Who had put the nation to shame
The failure of this unpleasant figure
Who had intelligence meagre
To enter the Royal Navy, his claim to fame.

At 8.30 am, a taxi headed for Birla House gate
Driving to the back of the Birla Estate.
Kistaya and Apte
Badge and Karkare
All set to eliminate a man great.

From there to the prayer ground they went
On shattering the peace malevolently bent.
Determination they didn't lack
Alas, he would be shot at the back
Soon the deceptive peace was all rent!

Bursting at the seams with an evil vigour
They were going to kill the half-naked figure
With deadly ammunition
And a diabolic fusion
Escaping amid the confusion it would trigger.

According to plan, they were well-disguised
Many a time their plans they had revised
With infinite care
Their revolvers they did repair
Not wanting to miss their target most prized.

Gandhi would now be the target of a frontal attack
In the earlier plan, he was to be shot at the back.
This was the conclusion
After whispered consultation
Among the conspirators who planned the attack.

At a tree Kistayya fired a shot
The defective revolver fell far short.
The birds fluttered
In irritation they muttered
Worried that they would be caught.

Newspapers flashed news of Gandhi's recovery
At Hindu Mahasabha building, Apte met Godse.
In a clump of trees
In the morning breeze
They tested their revolvers on that Tuesday!

Suddenly among the trees guards materialised
With suspicious eyes, the conspirators they sized
With dexterity quick
The minds sick
Hid the revolvers, their expressions disguised.

They were tourists the patrol party they told.
Falsehood held sway on that day cold.
They were on tenterhooks
Braving suspicious looks
Away went the party, their breaths they did hold.

Six hours later to the prayer ground he would walk
Unsuspecting, to his disciples he would talk.
But evil men at work
In ambush, did lurk
Their machinations entire nation would shock.

At Marine Hotel, they met for the last time
Minds deranged, fearful the clime.
They made eleventh hour preparations
Amidst suggestions and counter suggestions
To shoot the crusader, cacophonous the rhyme!

To hasten to the prayer ground they yearned
With a fire, their hearts burned
Now everything was set
It was no point to fret
That the tables could unexpectedly be turned.

At 5.10 pm Badge and Kistayya, their places took
Here and there, casting a surreptitious look.
They talked with Godse
Karkare and Apte
To complete their mission by hook or by crook!

Madanlal Pahwa, the twenty-year-old
The guncotton slab was all set to explode
Just a few feet away
On that fateful day.
Followed by grenades on the evening cold.

There was no panic, just the resounding echo
The murder attempt had been a fiasco.
There were sounds muffled
Gandhi was unruffled
He was seen pleading for the misguided foe!

He was only a tiny cog in the machine
There were many others behind the scene.
With wrath filled
They wanted Gandhi killed
For to the Muslims, he had partial been!

The apostle of nonviolence and truth
Harboured no ill-will against the youth
Who, Gandhi believed, was misguided.
Violence, Gandhi derided
Love he hoped could change the youth uncouth.

After the outrage, his security was tightened.
Unrestrained violence and hatred had heightened.
This man of no guile
Craved to face a bullet with a smile.
At the idea of going to Pakistan, he brightened.

He was depressed at the rampant profanity
And hoped to convince Jinnah of its futility.
As his health returned
With this fire he burned
On 27th he went to a mausoleum of great sanctity.

Which had been a victim of Hindu vandalism.
He was pained at the signs of barbarism
Of Khwaja Qutabuddin, screens were damaged
Hearts ravaged, and hopes savaged.
With an ardour great, he spoke of humanism.

Relations with Pakistan he wanted to mend
Rampant bloodshed he couldn't comprehend.
Within him a fire burned
To go to Pakistan he yearned
In the shadows lurked death, incomparable friend.

Not wanting to be a witness to the fratricidal strife
For lasting peace he could willingly stake his life
Chaotic was his mind
Ah—life was unkind
With portents grim, the environment was rife!

Across the Transvaal he had tirelessly walked
With a fistful of salt, an Empire he had rocked.
The indefatigable soul
Had to perform yet another role
At the authorities, a snook he had cocked.

The intrepid warrior in the mendicant's attire
Had reemerged, with a renewed fire.
Yearned the great Indian sage
To forge a bond with his message
Between India and Pakistan all afire!

Gandhi made himself very accessible to riot victims and all others who wanted to meet him. Some people who wanted him dead also tried to kill him when they met him

Love he had preached in many a village
A new power surged through his fragile image.
To Pakistan he wanted to go
This he wanted people to know
He was all set for this new pilgrimage.

...The Conspiracy

On 26th January at the Thane railroad station
At night a trio huddled together in consultation
Nathuram Godse insisted
And vehemently persisted
That alone he would carry out the assassination.

Trains trundled by, like nocturnal monsters.
In the yard the plan hatched the Gandhi haters.
It was Godse's decision
That in Gandhi's assassination
Gopal Godse would not be one of the conspirators.

It was indeed a problem formidable
That they did not own a revolver dependable.
Half the battle would be won
When they found one
And silenced the enemy indomitable.

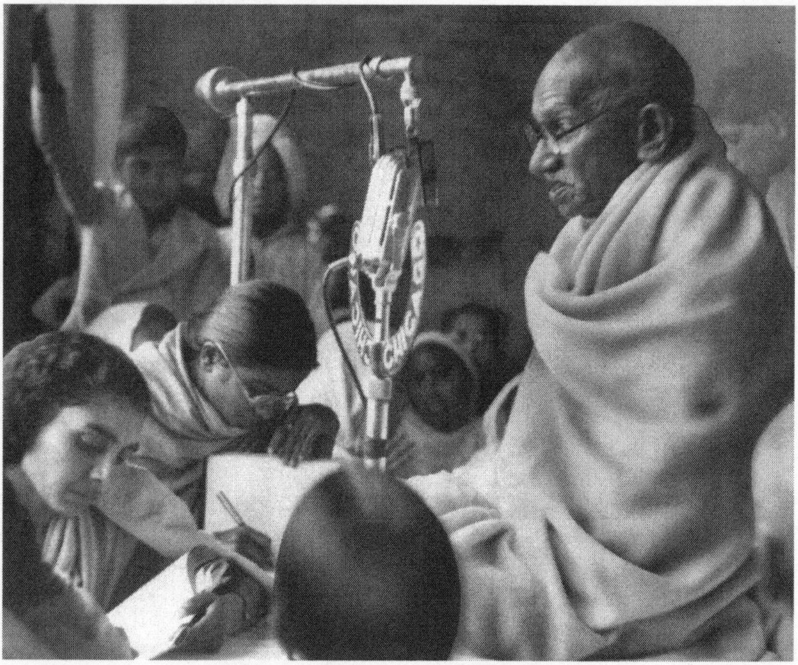

Gandhi preparing to address the nation

To meet in Delhi on the 29th was their decision.
They had tried to clear the cobwebs of confusion.
The venue was Birla Temple
They had time ample
To hunt for a revolver to carry out their intention.

On 27th morning while a chilly wind blew
Nathuram Godse and Apte to Delhi flew
To Gwalior they took a train
Shrugging off the strain
In search of a good revolver the conspirators two!

After a lot of haggling a revolver they procured
In its pursuit, a 400-mile detour they endured.
They had crossed a hurdle
Their blood did not curdle
Of success they were now reassured!

Now back to Delhi, Godse took a night train
Chaotic thoughts whirring in his brain.
By Apte accompanied
He did not feel weak kneed
Nor harassed by the undue strain.

Outside the Birla Temple, Karkare waited
Godse gave instructions in a mood elated.
With a fire he did burn
To Poona, Apte and Karkare should return
They had other responsibilities, he stated.

They moved into a retiring room at the station.
A day away was the assassination.
Round the corner was success
A wrong they longed to redress.
Later, Karkare and Apte went out for diversion.

The fateful morning after a breakfast light
They geared up for the imminent fight
His revolver Godse wanted to test
A man had to be put to eternal rest
They hired a tonga with anxiety slight.

Stopped near the woods and resolutely walked.
Deeply engrossed, Godse hardly talked.
He fired at a tree
His mind was not free
Satisfied with the revolver, now back they walked.

In the trees, the chilly breeze sloughed
Onward the conspirator ploughed.
No longer feeling tired
To Birla House he went in a tonga hired
It was quarter to five, the breeze still billowed.

People of different hues formed the congregation
To listen to one armed with moral ammunition
In anticipation, his skin tingled
With the people he mingled
Forging ahead with a vile determination.

Apte and Karkare reached there in minutes few
Godse needed the moral support of these men two.
On the day cold
The men bold
Merged into the crowd, and waited for the cue.

Gandhi was in a mood of calm elation
He smilingly faced the prayer congregation
Before the apostle of nonviolence
Godse bowed in reverence.
Between twin forces there would be a collision!

Towards each other were heading these forces two.
With a shove someone brushed past Manu.
Out of the crowd he lunged
Towards Gandhi he plunged
On the ground he hurled an astounded Manu.

The shades of the evening had begun to fall
Unaware the country of the tragedy about to befall.
On that day ill-fated
Some jostled, some prostrated
Ignorant of the brisk-footed gloomy pall.

With a resounding impact the two forces met
Soon the nation would lose its precious asset.
On that tragic day
When people were about to pray
The force swept forward to fire his first bullet.

The Last Day
30 January 1948

On this day of his life he had myriad fears.
His heart heavy with unshed tears.
Of death did he have a premonition?
He teetered on the brink of indecision.
Seized by a restlessness that was fierce.

3.30 am was his hour of greeting the morn.
Still recovering from the fast, he looked wan.
To him Manu was dear
Now he tweaked her ear
This ritual he followed at the crack of every dawn.

Manu chanted a hymn, *O man, do not rest.*
Many misgivings churned in his breast.
He was in an irascible mood.
The portents were not good.
Did he sense his departure from his earthly nest?

For cleansing the soul, prayer was his broom.
A ray of light in the all-encompassing gloom.
On a spirit un-calm
It acted as a balm.
Prayers over, Manu lead him into his room.

It was cold; she covered him with a wrap.
For half-an-hour he took a much-needed nap.
It was still dark
Outside, a dog did bark.
An early bird in the tree, its wings did flap.

Over the draft of free India's constitution he had worked.
Although very anxious and utterly irked.
His mind was muddled
In his wrap he huddled.
After the prayers he had slightly perked.

On his body the fast had taken a heavy toll.
But still in the garden, he took a stroll.
He felt strong enough.
Ah, life was tough.
Wanton despair had crept into his soul.

His brain was gripped with uncertainty.
Unsteadily, he tried to get a foothold on reality.
Although weak and jaded.
To the bathroom he went unaided.
On his shoulders, a heavy responsibility.

In the past, many a mile he had walked.
With powerful strides, the youth he had mocked.
In 1930, staff in hand.
With his seventy-eight-strong band
Had trudged 241 miles, the Empire had rocked!

Now his flesh was weak, though spirit willing.
In his mind a thousand thoughts milling.
Firm of step and clear eyed.
He had been the fatherly guide.
Unsteady of gait, pained by the rampant killing.

'Strange you look, walking by yourself', Manu said.
The Dandi-walker, cautiously did tread.
With this energy new
He took steps few.
Bapu was frail, Manu was filled with dread.

He had no flesh; he was only skin and bone.
'I look well, don't I? Walk alone, walk alone.'
He said with joy infantile.
Outwardly did Manu smile.
Inwardly, his lack of strength, she did mourn.

In Noakhali when inter-religious fire raged
To stem this violence a lone battle he had waged.
Blood for blood was the refrain
Gandhi was in immense pain.
He hunted for the divine in humanity deranged.

Walk alone, this refrain of Tagore's song
He had hummed while righting many a wrong.
Noakhali was in a shambles.
He had crossed filth and brambles.
With strides energetic and long.

Untiringly he walked from village to village
Spreading his message on the Noakhali pilgrimage
The area was inaccessible
With chilblained feet, the indomitable
Walked on, at seventy-seven years of age!

With Pyarelal he discussed conditions in Noakhali.
Spent time reading newspapers, learning Bengali.
He was under great strain
The grim scenario giving him pain
Pyarelal urged him to leave immediately for Noakhali.

Many a time he hinted at his approaching death
Which forged forward with wicked stealth.
Although physically poor
The man was a doer
Bursting at the seams with a unique moral wealth.

There were meetings and conferences galore
Into Birla House visitors unceasingly did pour.
Though usually incisive
He appeared unusually indecisive
In his talks with those who came to his door!

In the afternoon some letters he dictated
Off and on, his disciples he berated.
At his door
There were visitors more
In the wings, silently, another visitor waited.

He met De Silva from Ceylon, despite schedule tight
Also the photographer Margaret Bourke-White.
De Silva's daughter his autograph sought
To her, this mattered a lot.
Ahead surged the mysterious visitor, macabre his might!

His every step a victory of unadulterated guile.
The man of moral might had to walk many a mile.
The clock struck four
One person more
Was to be met some differences to reconcile.

Between Nehru and Patel there was friction
Filling Gandhi with unbearable tension.
In the stormy weather
They must hold together.
To Nehru he wrote, seeking his cooperation.

Both were skilled and absolutely capable
For the country purely indispensable.
Accompanied by his daughter, Patel came
To him, Gandhi said the same.
Towards the ground moved the man irrepressible.

With the sorry state of things displeased
Lines of impatience on his forehead creased
It was not a figment of the imagination
But in the absorbing conversation
He had forgotten the prayer time, ire increased.

Unpunctuality he could never brook.
His rosary, spittoon, spectacles and note book
With a spurt of vigour
Manu picked up this wealth meager
And to the ground a shortcut they took.

Followed by two Congressmen from Kathiawar
Who wanted a few minutes with this star.
In a mood worried
To the ground he hurried
Smilingly folded his hands in a Namaskar.

Fuming at the unprecedented delay
For which his walking sticks he tried to flay
Lovingly he talked
Briskly he walked
Unaware that he walked to his death that day.

Lifting his hands and joining them in a salutation
He apologised for the delay, in consternation.
Unseen by him a man edged forward
Was he a mad man or a coward?
He whipped out a pistol, with no compunction.

Three shots he fired in quick succession
Dumb-founded was the prayer congregation
In horror they gaped
This time Gandhi had not escaped
There were roars of grief and lingering confusion.

With 'Hey Ram' on his lips the titan fell
On the grass he lay, everything was pell-mell.
With the bullet third
His spectacles fell to the earth
His sandals slipped, things were unwell.

With a forgiving countenance, he breathed his last
A pall of gloom on the nation was cast
What an irony tragic
That a man so heroic
Should in this manner have breathed his last.

On their laps the girls cradled his head
With his blood, the earth becoming red.
By a wave of grief swept
People sobbed and wept
In dismay, filled with dread.

His face turned pale and thinner
While people pounced on the sinner.
The assassin had done his work
With grief the people went berserk
Cruel Death had defeated an interpid winner.

A cloud had snuffed out an effulgent sunray
Gandhi's meager wealth lay in disarray.
On this day cold and gray.
His earthly shackles he had shed.
A moral giant now lay dead.

'The light has gone out from Asia', Nehru wept.
The hearts of people to their mouths leapt.
Was the Mahatma no more
Had he really fallen a victim to gore?
People of all communities felt lost and bereft.

The lover of the cross had himself been crucified.
The people of his country lamented and sighed.
Filled with consternation
And a tumultuous passion
A bundle of bones, so fearlessly had died.

A labyrinthine queue walked past his room
Where he lay, oblivious to the encircling gloom.
Unendingly flew the tears
Mourning a loss fierce
Would a newborn nation hurtle towards doom?

Through tears, at the beloved face they gazed
At the forgiving expression, intensely amazed.
Not an eye was dry
As they bid goodbye
To the man, a victim of minds half-crazed!

To their leader a tearful farewell they bid
Some mourners valiantly their emotions hid.
Haters had stilled
A voice with love filled
He had forgiven them for what they did.

Through the window petals were showered at him.
Horizontal lay the vertical man in times grim.
Restive the crowd grew
In great agony was Nehru
With unshed tears his eyes grew dim.

Across the blue sky Dakotas streaked.
On the road many an old limb creaked.
They were in a daze
Though in a surreal haze
Wiping cheeks which were tear streaked.

The well-dressed, the ill-dressed, the unhealthy
The poor, the wealthy and also the healthy
As hearts converged
The rich and the poor merged
Dumb struck over the loss of a soul wealthy.

Joined together in a despair mute
With failing eye sight, the hopeless, the destitute
Their skin sagged
Their feet they dragged
Completely heartbroken by a tragedy absolute.

Heartbroken was grief-struck humanity
Utterly unable to understand the brutal reality.
Brows people mopped
The horses clip-clopped
The world reeling under this act of insanity!

Of humility and truthfulness a peculiar combination
To Pearl S Buck, this was another crucifixion.
Of a man so rare
So just and fair
Who had rocked the world with his moral perception.

His heart had stopped, his voice was stilled
Into many a heart a fire he had instilled
His adversaries were mighty
But this man of piety
With a solitary perseverance the earth had tilled.

King of England, Archbishop of Canterbury
Mourned the loss of an impoverished country.
Chang Kai-shek and President Truman
Rued the death of so fine a man
Nations shocked by the loss extraordinary.

The Dalai Lama of Tibet, the President of France
Dignitaries world over were in a trance.
In times of utter moral decadence
This man of nonviolence
Had towered over pygmies, commanding reverence.

Entities and non-entities equally did mourn
This human being who is rarely born
The ascetic little
With his frame brittle
Was a moral colossus in a world strife-torn!

Devdas, Gandhi's youngest son, was emotion choked
On seeing his father's body blood soaked.
He touched his arm
Which was still warm
Nehru hid his face in Bapu's clothes, tears cloaked.

The man who had yet to walk many a mile
Alas was still, on his face a serene smile.
Eternally he slept
While people wept
For the man who had lead a life sans guile.

On a pyre eight feet square, two feet high
He was placed amid many a sigh
At four forty-five pm Ramdas set fire
To his beloved father's pyre
The logs crackled and leapt into the sky.

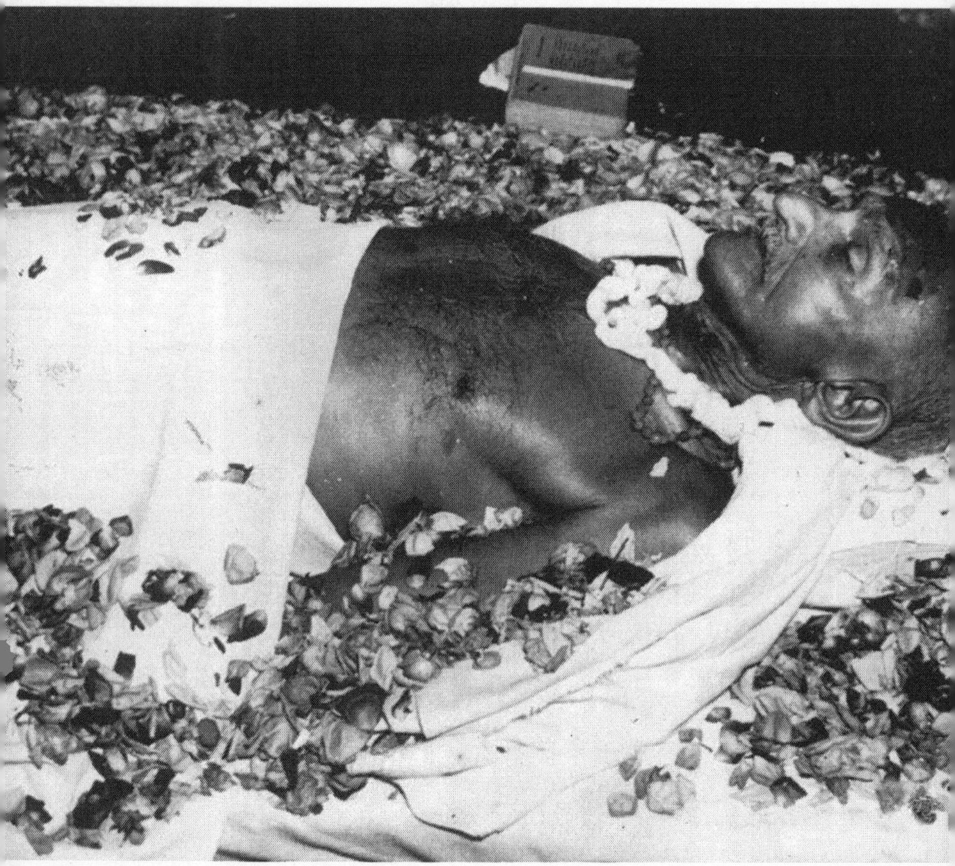

Journey of the Ashes

Shrugging away dust, he had always risen again
Now his dust lay in a special train
Composed of third class bogies freshly painted
The central wreath by floodlights illuminated
Which carried the ashes of the man cruelly slain.

Forward surged the mourners in reverence hushed
In an unending torrent tears gushed.
Mourning multitudes thronged this train.
Faces contorted in intense pain
In the rush people getting almost crushed.

For almost a mile they raced with the train
Their hearts burning with unbearable pain.
With dirt-laden feet
And with grief replete
People of every hue, crushed by the strain.

'Mahatma Gandhi ki jai' devastated lips thundered
With acute grief, hearts had been sundered
Was this step extreme
Just a bad dream
A nightmare into which they had blundered?

On 12th February 1948, the Sangam was packed
With mourners whose faces were wet, feet cracked.
Millions in stupor anguished
Grieved one who had perished
Hearts heavy with grief, bodies with sobs racked.

A remarkable saga had come to an end tragic.
Churchill's half-naked fakir for many was quixotic.
But now this man homeward bound
Mingling with the dust, immortality found.
The ordinary melded with extraordinary to emerge heroic.

Submariners

The thing is—in the name of what are we shedding all this blood? We've been told that the Germans attacked us, and the Germans in turn have been told that the Russians attacked them. The result was troops drawn up on the frontiers. Have you ever seen dogs being set on to fight? One is thrown at the other or their noses are poked together. The dogs start fighting tooth and nail, tearing lumps out of each other. That's what is happening to people. And it doesn't enter anyone's mind...

THE SEA BECKONS,1922-23
—Alexei Novikov-Priboi

To Kill a Mocking Bird

Mocking birds don't do one thing but make music for us to enjoy. They don't eat up people's gardens, don't nest in corn cribs, they don't do one thing but sing their hearts out for us. That's why it's a sin to kill a mockingbird.

—Harper Lee

Gandhi on Radio

Hitherto, nations have fought in manner of the brute. They have wreaked vengeance upon those whom they have considered to be their enemies... We in India have endeavoured to reverse the process. We feel that the law that governs brute creation... is inconsistent with human dignity. I personally would wait, if need be for ages, rather than seek to attain the freedom of my country through bloody means. I feel in the innermost recesses of my heart... that the world is sick unto death of blood-spilling. The world is seeking a way out and I flatter myself with the belief that perhaps it will be the privilege of the ancient land of India to show the way out to the hungering world...

It is a matter of deep humiliation to confess that we are a house divided against itself, that we Hindus and Mussulmans are flying at one another. It is a matter of still deeper humiliation that we Hindus regard several million of our own kith and kin as too degraded even for our touch.

—An excerpt from Gandhi's radio address, arranged by the Columbia Broadcasting Company of America, the day after Gandhi's arrival in England on 13 September 1931

The Mask of Anarchy

Gandhi once recited these verses to a Christian gathering in India.

Stand ye calm and resolute,
Like a forest close and mute,
With folded arms and looks which are
Weapons in unvanquished war.

And if then the tyrants dare,
Let them ride among you there,
Slash, and stab, and maim, and hew
What they like, that let them do.

With folded arms and steady eyes,
And little fear, and less surprise,
Look upon them as they slay
Till their rage has died away.

Then they will return with shame
To the place from which they came,
And the blood thus shed will speak
In hot blushes on their cheek.

Stand ye calm and resolute,
Like a forest close and mute,
With folded arms and looks which are
Weapons in unvanquished war.

And if then the tyrants dare,
Let them ride among you there,
Slash, and stab, and maim, and hew
What they like, that let them do.

With folded arms and steady eyes,
And little fear, and less surprise,
Look upon them as they slay
Till their rage has died away.

Then they will return with shame
To the place from which they came,
And the blood thus shed will speak
In hot blushes on their cheek.

Rise like lions after slumber
In unvanquishable number
Shake your chains to earth like dew
Which in sleep has fallen on you
Ye are many, they are few.

— ***Percy Bysshe Shelley***

Bibliography

1. Anthony J Parel, ed *Hind Swaraj* and Other writings, Cambridge University Press, 1997.
2. Azad, Abul Kalam, *India Wins Freedom,* New York: Longman Green and Co 1960.
3. Bhole LM, *Essays on Gandhian socio economic thought*, Delhi: Shipra publications, 2000.
4. Biswas SC (ed), *Gandhi Theory and Practice: Social Impact and Contemporary Relevance,* Simla: Indian Institute of Advanced Study, 1969.
5. Brown,Judith M, *Gandhi's Rise to Power,* Cambridge University Press, 1972.
6. Buch MA, *Rise and Growth of Indian Nationalism,* Atma Ram Printers Press, 1939.
7. Chakrabarti, Atulananda, *The Lonesome Pilgrim,* Allied Publishers, 1969.
8. Chandiwala Brij Krishna, *At the Feet of Bapu,* Navajivan Publishing House, 1954.

9. Collins Larry and Lapierre Dominique, *Freedom At Midnight,* Vikas Publishing House Pvt Ltd, 1976.
10. Dennis Dalton, *Gandhi's Power: Nonviolence in Action*, OUP 2001.
11. Doke Joseph J, *MK Gandhi,* Bhartiya Sarva Seva Sangh Prakashan, 1909.
12. Durga Das, *India From Curzon to Nehru and After,* Rupa and Co, 1973.
13. Fischer Louis, *The Essential Gandhi, An anthology of his writings on his life, work and ideas*, Vintage, 1992.
14. Fischer Louis, *The Life of Mahatma Gandhi,* Jonathan Cape 1957.
15. Fischer Louis (ed), *The Essential Gandhi,* George Allen and Unwin Ltd 1963.
16. Gandhi MK, *Village Swaraj*, Navjivan Publishing House 1959.
17. Gandhi MK, *From Yervada Mandir,* Navajivan Publishing Hosue, 1945.
18. Gandhi MK, *Communal Unity*, edited by Bharatan Kumarappa, Navajivan Publishing House 1949.
19. Gandhi MK, *My Religion*, edited and compiled by Bharatan Kumarappa, Navajivan Publishing House 1958.
20. Gandhi MK, *All Religions Are True*, edited by Anand T Hingorani, Pearl Publications 1962.
21. Gandhi MK. *The Way to Communal Harmony*, edited by UA Rao, Navajivan Publishing House 1963.
22. Ghosh Sudhir, *Gandhi's Emissary,* Rupa and Co 1967.

23. Hutchins FG, *Spontaneous Revolution – The Quit India Movement,* Manohar Book Service 1971.
24. Homer Jack, *The Gandhi Reader: A Source Book of His Life & Writings*, Grove Press 1956.
25. Markovits Claude, *The Ungandhian Gandhi: The life & after life of The Mahatma*, Anthem Press 2004.
26. Mahadev Desai, *The diary of Mahatma Gandhi*, Navjivan Publishing House 1948.
27. Nojeim Michael J, *Gandhi and King*, Greenwood Publishing Group 2004.
28. Nirmal Kumar Bose, *Selections from Gandhi*, Navjivan Publishing House, 1948.
29. Nanda BR, *Mahatma Gandhi* George Allen and Unwin Ltd, London, 1965.
30. Payne Robert, *The Life and Death of Mahatma Gandhi*, 1998.
31. Pyarelal, *Towards New Horizons*, Navjivan Publishing House, 1959.
32. Pyarelal, *Mahatma Gandhi – The Last Phase*, Nanajivan Publishing House, 1956, vol I Book-One and Book-Two, 2nd ed, 1966.
33. Polak HSL, Brailsford HN and Pethick- Lawrence, *Mahatma Gandhi,* Odhams Press Ltd, London, 1949.
34. Ravindra Kumar (ed) *Mahatma Gandhi At The Close of Twentieth Century*, Anmol 2004.
35. Raghavan N Iyer, *The Moral and Political thought of Mahatma Gandhi*, OUP 1973.
36. Trivedi Lisa, *Clothing Gandhi's Nation, Homespun and Modern*

India, Indiana University Press, 2007.

37. Tendulkar DG, *Mahatma,*: Government of India Publications Division, 1969, 8 vols.
38. Weber Thomas, *Gandhi as Disciple and Mentor*, Cambridge University Press 2004.
39. Weber Thomas, *Gandhi Gandhism & Gandhians*, Roli Books Pvt Ltd 2006.